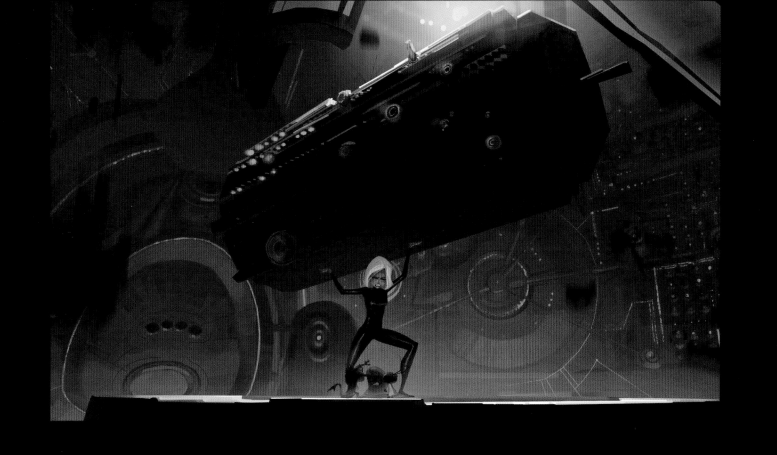

DREAMWORKS®

The Art of

MONSTERS VS ALIENS™

Foreword by Stephen Colbert

Text by Linda Sunshine

NEWMARKET PRESS
NEW YORK

FIRST EDITION

10 9 8 7 6 5 4 3 2 1

ISBN: 978-1-55704-824-0 (hardcover)

Library of Congress Catalog-in-Publication Data available upon request.

QUANTITY PURCHASES
Companies, professional groups, clubs, and other organizations may qualify
for special terms when ordering quantities of this title. For information, write to Special
Sales, Newmarket Press, 18 East 48th Street, New York, NY 10017; call (212) 832-3575 or
1-800-669-3903; FAX (212) 832-3629; or e-mail info@newmarketpress.com.

www.newmarketpress.com

Manufactured in the United States of America.

Special thanks to writer Linda Sunshine and designer Timothy Shaner
at Night and Day Design (nightanddaydesign.biz).

Produced by Newmarket Press: Esther Margolis, President and Publisher;
Frank DeMaio, Production Director; Keith Hollaman, Executive Editor;
Linda Carbone, Editor; Paul Sugarman, Digital Supervisor

Other Newmarket Pictorial Moviebooks and Newmarket Insider Film Books include:

CONTENTS

UNCLASSIFIED

Foreword **7**
by Stephen Colbert

Introduction **9**
Bringing the Characters to Life 11
Size and Scale 14
Style 16
The 3-D Initiative 17

PART ONE:
Character Design **19**
Susan aka Ginormica 20
Dr. Cockroach 28
The Missing Link 34
B.O.B. 42
Insectosaurus 50
Gallaxhar 56
Gallaxhar's Clones 63
Robots 64
President Hathaway 70
General W. R. Monger and Other Humans 74

PART TWO:
Locations **79**
Modesto, California 81
First Contact 84
Area Fifty-Something 93
Monster Prison 97
The War Room 103
San Francisco 108
The Mothership: Exterior 116
The Mothership: Interior 125
Capture, Extraction, and Cloning Devices 132

PART THREE:
Special F/X **143**
Exploding Planet 145
First Contact F/X 146
The Force Field and the Robot Beam 148
Taking Down the Golden Gate Bridge 151
Insectosaurus Snot 156
The Extraction Chamber 157
Mothership Destruction 160
Props: Military Vehicles, Tanks, and Guns 164
Clothes 169

PART FOUR:
The Making of
Monsters vs. Aliens **171**
Rigging and Animating 173
Surfacing and Lighting 176
Working in 3-D 180

PART FIVE:
Out of the Picture **183**
Mothballed Characters and Locations 185

Acknowledgments 192

(previous page) **First Contact**—Ritche Sacilioc—digital paint. *(above)* **Space**—Richard Daskas—digital paint.

SUBJECT: Foreword
AGENT: Stephen Colbert
STATUS: President of the
United States, Voice

I may not know much about art, but I know what I like:

Science Fiction.

When I was ten, I discovered that my family's attic was a doorway to The Future. Among the dusty Christmas decorations and broken lampshades were cardboard boxes stuffed with pulp Science Fiction novels and short story collections from the 1950s that my two eldest brothers had left behind when they had gone off to college and marriage and jobs. There were stacks of stories by C. M. Kornbluth, John W. Campbell, A. E. van Vogt, Henry Kutner, Alfred Bester, Keith Laumer, Cordwainer Smith, Robert A. Heinlein, Isaac Asimov, and Arthur C. Clarke. This was The Future as imagined by the past, and I was eager to go back and see It.

For years, these books became my refuge from reality. Inside their covers were worlds distant and dangerous. But what first drew me in was what was on their covers: Richly Colored Tomorrow. These cover paintings were mini-masterpieces of strange, sometimes surreal landscapes, on which spaceships with rounded bellies and needle noses balanced on Cadillac tail fins, their spindly ladders extended to the alien world below, while the bubble-helmeted hero descended to adventure or possible death at the hands of the multi-eyed, multi-armed, multi-mouthed creature that only we could see hiding behind the rock at the bottom of the picture.

(Also in The Future, we would evidently all be very fit and wear much tighter clothing, if these pictures were to be trusted. And I did trust them. Thirty years later, I am still waiting to get a six-pack on my stomach and a jetpack on my back.)

Science Fiction swallowed me whole. I would sneak these books into school and hide them behind my textbooks in class, but evidently not very well, because book after book was confiscated. Somewhere there is a retired math teacher with a great pulp collection. Or, as is sadly more likely, they all went into the trash. I miss those books, not really for the stories—those words have been reprinted in different editions and collections—but for all that cover art that is gone.

Gone, not just out of print but out of style. In the 1970s there was a revolution in our Future. The sleek, hypodermic V2 hulls of the prototypical space rockets were supplanted in the post–Apollo Mission world by "realistic" spaceships with angular lines and prows as blunt as a garbage barge and hulls craggy with slate gray apparatus.

This less romantic, mechanical vision of the future has at times been made colder by the use of digital design. But, to me, the art of *Monsters vs. Aliens* looks like it is reaching back to the softer, painterly style I remember from those early visions of our future. I see it in the curve of the invading alien hulls, the warmth of Ginormica's skin, and the rich blue of B.O.B.'s ...jelly?

The art of *Monsters vs. Aliens* seems both new and old at the same time. I think the best Science Fiction is that way, too. It invites us with the familiar and then surprises with worlds we've never imagined.

I'm happy for the ten-year-old boy or girl who finds it.

F or any animated feature, the journey from idea to finished film can take years and involve the creative input of innumerable people. *Monsters vs. Aliens* is no exception. Here is a 3-D movie that started life as two separate but somewhat related ideas.

By the fall of 2005, director Conrad Vernon had completed work on *Shrek 2* and was developing an idea for DreamWorks about a group of monsters. The concept was to parody the monster movies of the 1950s that Vernon loved as a kid. With an art director and an artist, he was trying to visualize a movie based on iconic horror-movie characters. "We were working on the look of the movie for about six months but didn't know what to do with the story," admits Vernon.

Around the same time, in another office on the DreamWorks Animation campus in Glendale, California, *Shark Tale* director Rob Letterman was considering his next project. He wanted to make a comedic, animated version of *The Dirty Dozen*, one of his all-time favorite movies. He pitched his idea to DreamWorks Animation CEO Jeffrey Katzenberg. It didn't go as he had planned. Instead, Katzenberg suggested that Rob meet Conrad to marry *The Dirty Dozen* idea with the monster concept.

Almost immediately, Vernon and Letterman connected artistically and quickly pulled together an outline that merged both of their ideas.

"We took a crack at pushing the story through the point of view of the monsters themselves and following the basic *Dirty Dozen* template of the monsters being called upon to save the world," says Letterman.

The idea seemed to have legs. Production designer David James worked on the project from almost the beginning and was immediately intrigued by the possibilities of the concept. "When I first started working on *Monsters vs. Aliens,* the

(left) **Monsters Released**—Michael Isaak—digital paint.

monsters were still in flux and the story had not been found yet," says James. "But I saw this as a sci-fi joke-making machine with huge potential for humor and visual fun. Here was the ultimate geek-out, adolescent boy fantasy."

Though they had the basic premise of what would eventually become *Monsters vs. Aliens*, it would take a lot of work—hundreds of ideas and story concepts and thousands of illustrations—to mold that premise into a workable presentation.

To start, if their monsters were going to save the world, they needed a worthy opponent, a villain that could match the extraordinary power and size of the monsters. They decided on an alien invader. But what kind of alien? What would it look like? And why was this alien such a threat to the world?

For Letterman, one particular image of an

alien invader was so visually compelling that it convinced him they had a workable idea for a movie.

This image of a mosquito-like alien was created by visual development artist Patrick Hanenberger. "This is the very first piece of art I did on the movie," says Hanenberger. "I had just come from a meeting with David [James]. We wanted to pitch an idea that invading aliens were here to suck the planet dry; they wanted our oil, water, and all our other natural resources. We came up with this idea of a giant mosquito and this crude drawing was an attempt to quickly capture that concept. It's just a quick sketch and somewhat out of perspective but I was going for the look of an early special effects shot from a cheesy B movie."

Crude or not, the drawing crystallized the

movie for Letterman. "This is one of the first pieces of art that came down the pike. This is very, very early on," says the director. "It's always interesting to me to see how we start with the early abstract ideas and how that refines itself to the finished piece. For the layman, this might not look like anything, but for me it shows how the entire movie is all going to happen. As a filmmaker I am keying in on the basic composition and lighting. This image shows me the pure conceit of the initial idea."

With the idea of the alien taking shape, the story had a villain, but it lacked a central hero.

Vernon and Letterman had narrowed the monsters down to five basic characters: a 49-foot-11-inch woman, a half cockroach/half human, an enormous insect, a mass of gelatinous goo, and a prehistoric fish/ape/human. In the begin-

(above left) **Early Oil Sucking Robots**—Patrick Hanenberger—digital paint. *(above right)* **Early Mosquito Robots**—Patrick Hanenberger—pencil.

ning, the monsters were all more or less of equal importance and the story was told through the voice of various characters—at times a therapist, a monster hunter, or a self-help guru named Tip Sommers. The movie opened with the scene called "First Contact," where the aliens land on Earth. Then it moved to "The War Room" where the president and his advisors decide to use the monster prisoners to fight the aliens. The monsters are introduced, and from there the story is told through the monsters' point of view.

But something wasn't working. There were too many monsters and too many points of view.

"We had the five basic characters but we needed to pick one to tell the story through," explains Letterman. "We felt that Susan was the one the audience could identify with most strongly. She starts off as a human and goes through a pretty compelling emotional journey, so we gravitated towards her as our central character. We decided to start with her origins, tell the story from her point of view, surround her with our other monsters, and figure out ways to get their basic emotional arcs tied into hers. We did a two-week blitz and outlined the story with her as our hero."

In this version, instead of opening with the aliens landing, the movie began with Susan's wedding, her contact with the flying meteor, her capture and imprisonment in the monster prison. The audience needed to know Susan if the story was going to be hers to tell.

Satisfied with their new outline, the team presented the concept.

Monsters vs. Aliens got the green light and went into full-scale production as the first movie authored specifically in 3-D by DreamWorks Animation.

BRINGING THE CHARACTERS TO LIFE

Making Susan the central character focused the story and gave the movie a female heroine. "It was a seminal moment when Susan became the hero of the story. Everyone was interested in a female heroine," says producer Lisa Stewart, who came to the project with live-action producing experience and expertise. "We as the audience are with her as she emerges, and we relate more to her than a cockroach."

In fact, for Stewart, it was seeing an early portrait of Susan that first piqued her interest in the movie. "It's rare to find a female heroine in an action-oriented animated film," says Stewart. "That image of Susan sitting on the roof of the gas station by Timothy Lamb is right after her fiancé Derek has dumped her, and she's taking stock of what her life was once and what it has now become. It's a very evocative image that says to me that this woman has found herself in an extraordinary situation and is trying to cope. It's like Edward Hopper meets *Mad* magazine. I want to spend time in that world and find out what happens to the character. Through all the many iterations of our story, we've always known this moment, this image, needs to be in the film."

Susan's story arc is an evolution of empowerment. At the start of the movie something extraordinary happens to her, but she initially rejects the idea of being unique. She keeps hoping she will shrink in size and go back to the life she was living. Through the course of the movie, Susan will come to embrace her uniqueness and transform from being small on the inside to being big in every way.

The other characters in the story will go along for the ride and discover their own inner strengths. "Ideally, every character in the ensemble has a defining moment," says Peter Ramsey, head of story. "All the monsters are colorful characters with rich back stories. But when centering the movie on Susan, you can only give them so much screen time without distracting from her story. Everything about their story has to thematically resonate with Susan's story. We had to make the movie more about her growth and discovering herself as opposed to her learning to fit in with a cast of misfits."

An enormous amount of work, energy, and

thought went into creating each of the characters in the movie. And once the creative team had captured the basic look and emotional register of each character, the actors hired for voice work helped define the characters in their recording sessions. "We were fortunate in our casting in that each actor has really added something to the character," says Lisa Stewart. "Everyone embraced and helped define their respective characters. Reese's charm and intelligence are obvious. Seth brings his own wide-eyed enthusiasm to B.O.B. Hugh Laurie actually is that erudite. Will Arnett invests The Missing Link with his great, raw sense of humor. And with Stephen, Keifer, Rainn and

Paul Rudd, we've been graced with a tremendous cast."

SIZE AND SCALE

All of the creative people working on this movie agree that next to creating a movie in 3-D, the biggest challenge in making *Monsters vs. Aliens* was the issue of size and scale. "In most movies, you have three or four characters talking to each other at the same level but that was not the case in our movie," says David James. "This created all kinds of issues. For example, in the beginning we had an idea to have a monster group hug. But then we realized you can't hug a 400-foot monster! All you get to see is a toe."

From the very start, scale and proportion had to be factored into every design decision. "Scale is what makes our movie so unique," says Lisa Stewart. "We have a 49-foot-11-inch Susan, a 400-foot robot, a 350-foot Insectosaurus, outer space, and the Golden Gate Bridge."

The first step was creating a line-up that represented the scale of every character in the story.

Since the characters live in an environment, everything around them—houses, office buildings, interior spaces—had to be proportionate to their size. "Selling that sense of scale is essential in this movie," explains art director Michael Isaak. "We had to focus on the volume and size of locations."

(previous page) **Susan At Gas Station 2**—Timothy Lamb—digital paint. *(above)* **Robots Invade**—Ritche Sacilioc—digital paint.

The dynamics of the film required that every set had to be both intimate and huge, two concepts that are usually diametrically opposed. If your character is 300-feet tall, you won't see all of him until you are a quarter-mile away. And how do you contain such a huge creature into a space like a holding cell without losing the sense of his size?

"Caricature people need to live in a caricature environment or else they look freakish," says David James. "We had to proportion everything they use and everything they interact with."

At the same time, the filmmakers had to make sure they did not stray too far away from being funny. Even though this movie is about monsters and a scary, all-out alien invasion, it is a comedy. "Much of the design was geared to let people know they could laugh," explains David James. "When you see an entire army gathered in front of the robot, how do you know you can laugh? Well, you look at the silliness of the robot and the shape and character."

Every design was focused on both its purpose in the movie and the idea behind it that made it work in the film. "We were looking at finding out what was funny about a spaceship or what was in the shape that could be exaggerated, caricatured or cartooned while at the same time retaining a sense of purpose or danger," says James. "It's an incredible balancing act. If it goes too far to the goofy, it falls out of the realm of the threatening. But if it is too threatening, than it falls out of the realm of our movie."

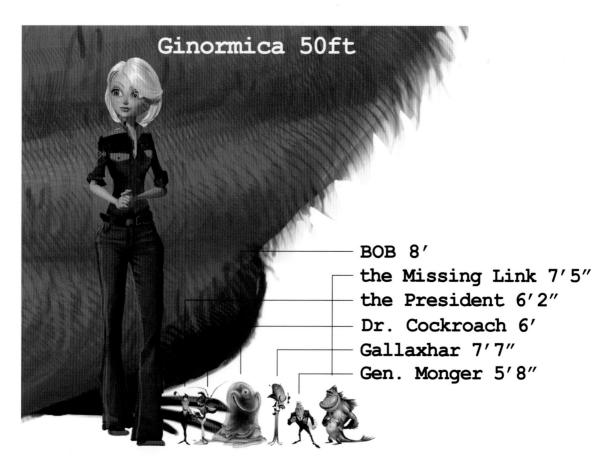

Ginormica 50ft

BOB 8'
the Missing Link 7'5"
the President 6'2"
Dr. Cockroach 6'
Gallaxhar 7'7"
Gen. Monger 5'8"

(top) **Monster Line-Up**—Timothy Lamb—digital paint—Ronald Kurniawan—digital paint—Craig Kellman, Devin Crane—character design. *(bottom)* **Robot vs. Jets**—Patrick Hanenberger—digital paint.

STYLE

Originally, the idea for the look of the movie was to parody the cheesy monster movies from the 1950s but filtered through a sophisticated contemporary lens. This meant there wouldn't be any of the amateurish set designs or poor camera work that typically characterizes those beloved mid-century, low-budget movies. The movie is meant to look like today, not the 1950s, so the challenge was to be reminiscent of those films without really looking like them.

The actual style of the film changed dramatically during the course of production. At first, both the characters and the environments had an exaggerated and cartoon-like feel but that quickly changed. "Our early art was more cartoony, more stylized," says art director Scott Wills. "Then the style of the movie started becoming more realistic because cartoony didn't really sell the story."

The filmmakers made a cinematic decision that the movie would have the quality of a live-action film. "For the comedy to work, it had to play against the real world," says head of layout Damon O'Beirne. "We also wanted to create the live-action feel of an adrenaline-rushed action movie."

The final visual concept was to render the environments and light them to look as realistic as possible, but to then add a subtle spin on the actual shapes of the buildings. "Look closely (at the buildings) and the windows are bent," says Rob Letterman. "The shape language has that exaggerated, skewed character feel. But the surfacing, lighting, and photography elements are very real."

The idea was simple. Apply the basic guidelines of shooting a live-action movie to the creation of an animated one. "We used a multi-camera approach and shot lots of coverage for every shot, the same way we would shoot live

(above) **Monger In War Room**—Scott Wills—digital paint. *(above right)* **SF Buildings**—Rachel Tiep-Daniels, Brett Nystul—3D design.

action," says O'Beirne. Even though animated camera work allows for almost any conceivable shot or angle, on *Monsters vs. Aliens* the filmmakers confined themselves within the general restrictions of shooting with a camera on a set. "The conceit of our cinematography style is to shoot this animated feature as if it were a live-action film," says Letterman. "If you couldn't get a shot on a live-action film with your equipment, we didn't include it."

THE 3-D INITIATIVE

As if the filmmakers didn't have enough challenges in bringing this idea to fruition, they were also challenged with making this film in 3-D stereoscopic. (3-D stereoscopic refers to the kind of movie that requires polarized glasses, as opposed to a 3-D animated feature that creates images in the computer. The differences are detailed later on in this book.) In this case, DreamWorks Animation's state-of-the-art, proprietary authoring tools combined with the latest Intel technology, resulting in a more immersive 3-D experience called InTru 3D.

The fact that the filmmakers were focused on shooting in a realistic style and keeping everything within the proper scale and proportion proved to be a blessing, as the 3-D technology required exactly those elements to work.

"The scale was so huge, we had to design a lot more than we thought we would,"

says David James. "And because of the scale, we couldn't cheat it the way we can with smaller scale. Matte painting, for example, was relegated to sky and far distances so it didn't look like Flintstone background."

Another example was in the heat waves and ripple effects when a jet flies by. "In 3-D stereoscopic we needed to create a whole new technique for the ripple effect," says Ken Bielenberg, visual effects supervisor. "We also had to find a balance to make sure that if something was exploding it was a 'wow' moment, but not a moment like throwing a spear at the audience. That would feel deliberate and take the audience out of the movie."

"The simplest way to think about making a 3-D movie is that you have to make one movie for each eye," says Phil McNally, stereoscopic supervisor for *Monsters vs. Aliens*. "In real life if you close one eye and hold out your finger, when you look at it with one eye and then the other, there is a shift. With each eye, your finger is in a different position compared to the background. That is what we have to create with our left movie and our right movie."

The first two scenes created in 3-D for *Monsters vs. Aliens* were "First Contact," where the aliens land on Earth and are greeted by the president, and "The War Room," where the president and his top advisors come together to decide what to do about the invasion.

Once everyone saw how the 3-D worked on these two scenes, it was clear that the technology and story were a perfect fit. While most 3-D movies play to the technology and use sight gags to highlight what 3-D can do, that was not the directive here. Everything in this movie is BIG and 3-D makes it feel BIG. No one could ask for more—the technology works to enhance the story without becoming the story. Here, the 3-D initiative allows the audience to sink into the experience of the movie and enter a BIG, BIG world.

(*above*) **CG character art**.

PART ONE

CHARACTER DESIGN

HELL HATH NO FURY LIKE

GINORMICA!!

A WOMAN SPURNED AND A CITY in PANIC!!

In the beginning, the Susan character was just one of the many monsters featured in the movie. She was conceived as a very tall and rather sexy woman in skimpy clothes. "Originally, she was like a 1950s bombshell B-movie girl," says character designer Craig Kellman.

Then the focus of the movie switched and Susan became the central character, the hero through whom the story is told. This gave Susan more importance and responsibility. Once Susan's character became clearer, so did her look. "We went toward a more innocent, cute, and somewhat modern look," says Craig Kellman.

Like all of the humans in the movie, Susan is a caricature. Although she is a modern woman, as a caricature, many of her traits—both physical and personality-wise—are meant to be exaggerations that are grounded in reality. The job of the filmmakers was to first figure out who she was and then use those elements of her style and emotional make-up to create a caricature of Susan Murphy.

A huge amount of time, energy, and talent was invested in exploring Susan's proportions, her hair, and facial features, in an effort to dig out her character. "She is our main character, so we left no visual stone unturned," says David James. Like every human character in the movie, her looks and proportions are meant to be caricatures, to exaggerate particular visual aspects in order to show us who she really is.

Susan is the most normal of all the human characters in the story. The story requires her to be both appealing and refined. While the males in the movie have huge, disproportionately long heads, making them look rather like bubble-heads, Susan's head is wide instead of long. Thus, she has a different distortion from the men in the movie. Yes, she is stylized and somewhat cartoony, but she is still a girl we can relate to.

When Rob Letterman and Conrad Vernon approached Reese Witherspoon to give voice to the character, they tried to stress the importance of having a female heroine in the starring role. "We told Reese we wanted to do something different and unique, and we wanted Susan to balance out the dudes in the film," says Rob. "When Reese heard that, she just lit up."

The movie opens on Susan's wedding day, when she is suddenly hit by a meteor and splashed by alien goop, which causes her to grow into Ginormica. After literally busting out of her church, Susan is whisked away to a holding cell at an undisclosed government location, where she meets several other monsters.

Our heroine weighs around 23,640 pounds and is 49 feet, 11 inches tall. She's big, she's beautiful, and she's impervious to nuclear and atomic energy.

Can she learn to love her new life?

(previous pages) **Susan Expressions**—Devin Crane—pencil. (opposite) **Ginormica Poster**—Timothy Lamb—digital paint.

(top) **Susan's Prom**—Ronald Kurniawan—digital paint. (bottom) **Susan Mini-Golfing**—Timothy Lamb—digital paint.

Susan was meant to look like a vintage 1940s starlet with those big Bette Davis eyes. Her features are extreme but she is still pretty.

—DEVIN CRANE, CHARACTER DESIGNER

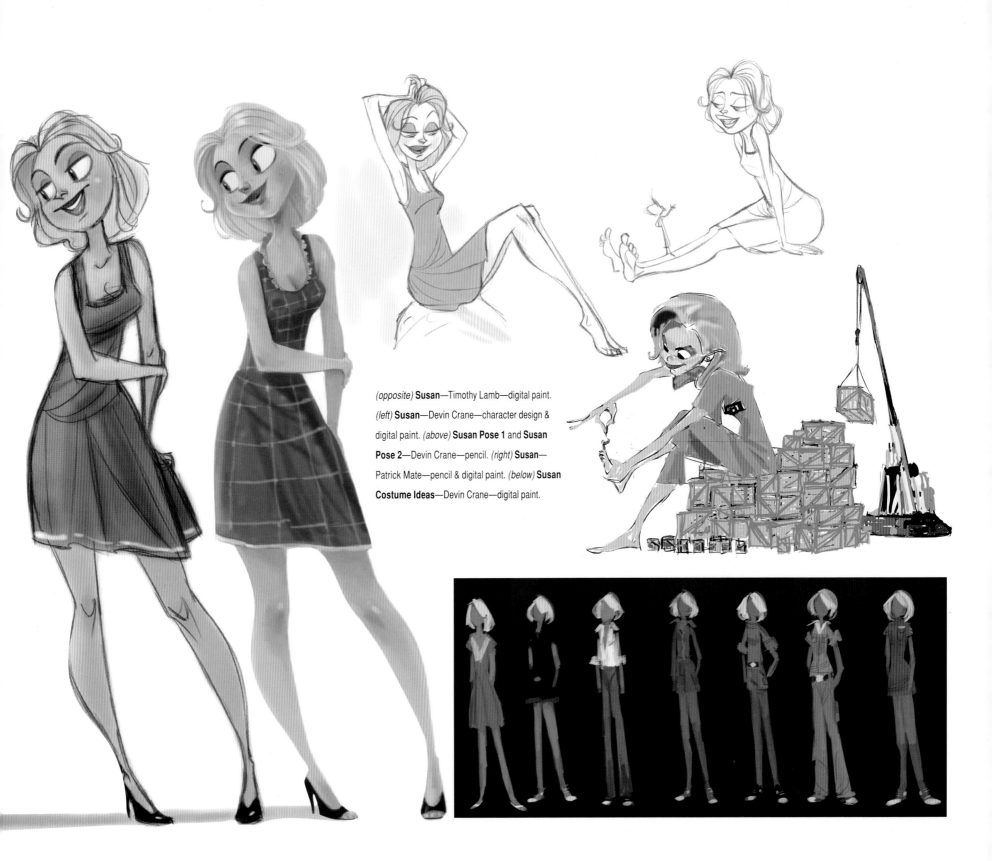

(opposite) **Susan**—Timothy Lamb—digital paint.
(left) **Susan**—Devin Crane—character design & digital paint. *(above)* **Susan Pose 1** and **Susan Pose 2**—Devin Crane—pencil. *(right)* **Susan**—Patrick Mate—pencil & digital paint. *(below)* **Susan Costume Ideas**—Devin Crane—digital paint.

(above) **Susan On Building**—Craig Kellman—pencil. (left) **Susan On Building**—Craig Kellman—character design—Sam Michlap—digital paint. (below) **Susan**—Devin Crane—digital paint.

CRAIG KELLMAN

(above) **Susan's Wedding Day**—Patrick Hanenberger—digital paint—Rachel Tiep-Daniels—3d design. *(below)* **Susan Kid Photo 1, 2** and **3**—Ronald Kurniawan—pencil & digital paint.

(left) **Battle Susan**—David James—digital paint. *(above)* **Susan and Insecto**—Craig Kellman—pencil—Richard Daskas—digital paint.

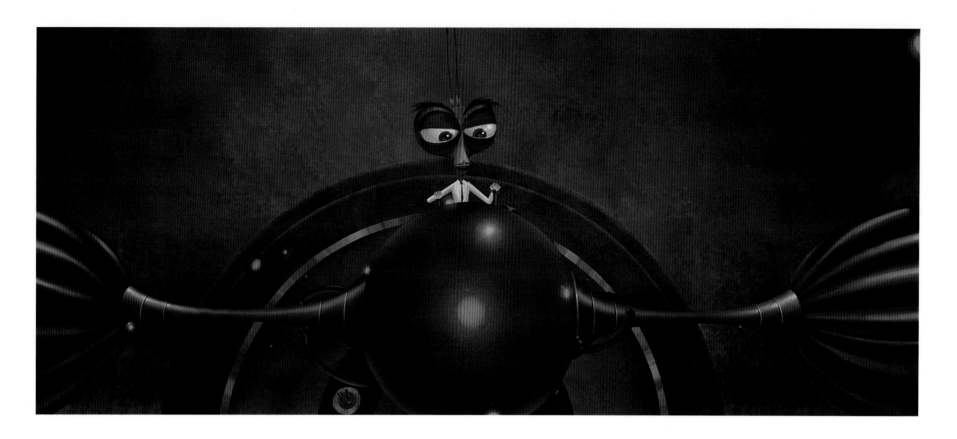

Dr. Cockroach is the mad-scientist/genius who tried to combine the indestructibility of the cockroach with human characteristics. He experimented on himself and became a guy with a giant cockroach head. "We wanted to give Dr. Cockroach a kind of James Mason style, make him elegant and erudite but with a disgusting head and hideous insect habits," says Craig Kellman. "He's a scientist and very together and articulate, but the cockroach part of him can't stop himself from slurping soup or licking sugar off the sidewalk."

While the designers agonized over the look for Susan, Dr. Cockroach "was the easiest character to create," says Conrad Vernon. "The mad scientist is a staple of horror movies. We started with that, took out some of the more obvious elements, and added some dimension."

Dr. Cockroach has a disproportionately huge head—perhaps to point out that he has a disproportionately huge brain. Yet his body is much smaller and more delicate in scale than his head. "This was meant to emphasize the absolute incongruity of his character," explains David James. "He is refined and dignified in the way he talks and walks but he also consumes garbage. We wanted the two visuals (his head and his body) to be as diametrically opposed as possible."

In almost every major scene, Dr. Cockroach is called up to invent something or otherwise use his extraordinary brain to help his fellow monsters.

Though he rises to the challenge, his inventions inevitably suffer from some fatal flaw. "They're brilliant inventions, but one thing always goes wrong," explains Vernon. "He creates the trolley car in the San Francisco scene, but forgets to put brakes in it."

With his perfect posture, Dr. Cockroach stands tall to exemplify that he is proud and full of self-importance. He is a doctor, albeit a doctor of literature, but he still wears a lab coat to convince us of his genius. "But there is a mad side to him," adds Vernon. "He doesn't mind having a cockroach head and can't understand why anyone else would. To him, it's a small price to pay to survive a nuclear holocaust."

(*opposite*) **Dr. Cockroach Poster**—Timothy Lamb—digital paint. (*above*) **Dr. C**—Richard Daskas—digital paint.

DR. COCKROACH PHD

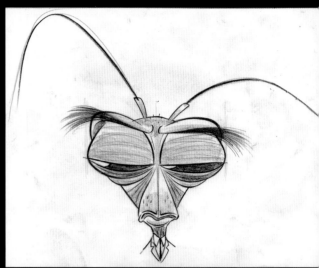

(*above and below*) **Dr. Cockroach**—Craig Kellman—pencil.
(*left*) **Dr. Cockroach**—JJ Villard—color pencil.
(*opposite*) **Dr. Cockroach**—Craig Kellman—pencil.

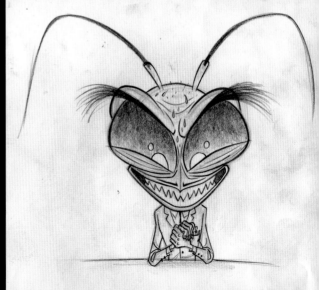

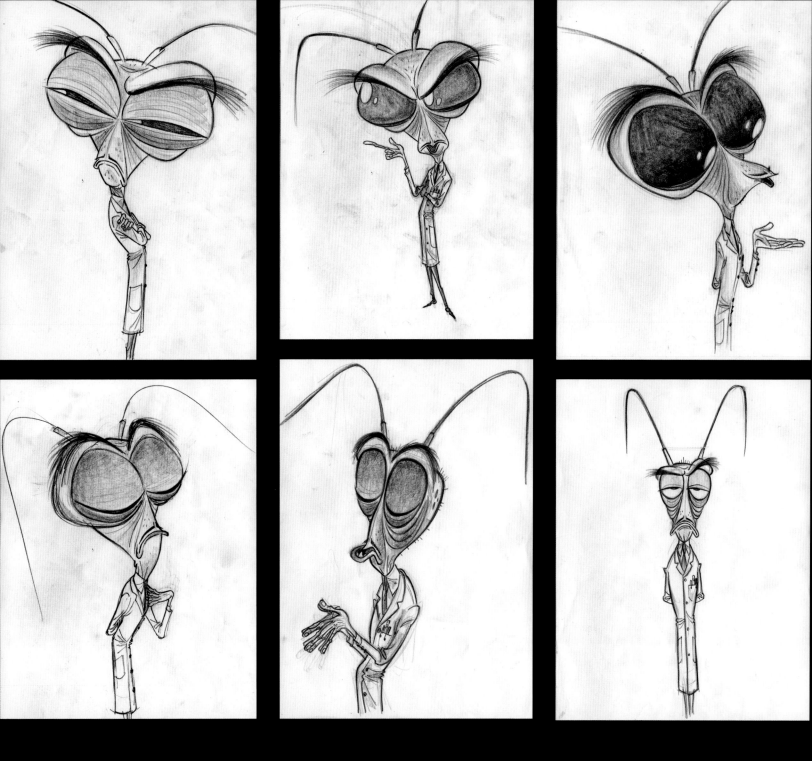

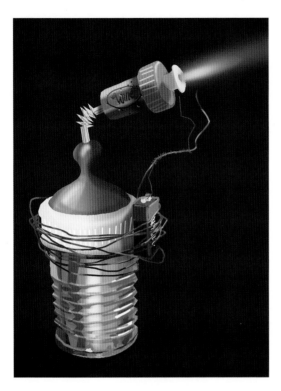

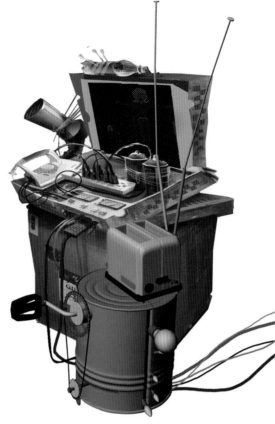

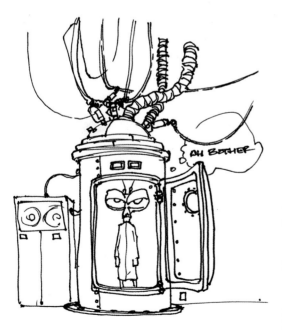

(*above left*) **Blowtorch**—Michael Isaak—digital paint.
(*above right*) **Shrinking Machine**—Rachel Tiep Daniels,
Michael Isaak—3D design—Timothy Lamb—digital paint.
(*left*) **Dr. Cockroach**—David James—pencil. (*right*) **Dr. C's
Computer**—David James—layout—Timothy Lamb—digital paint.

At one point in the story development,
Dr. Cockroach builds a computer
out of found objects and my
favorite visual joke is that he
uses a mouse for the mouse.
—DAVID JAMES, PRODUCTION DESIGNER

The Missing Link is literally the prehistoric link between early man and our underwater predecessors. As an ancient fish, The Missing Link decided one day to try living on land. Unfortunately, he emerged at the height of the Ice Age, so he froze solid and had to wait 20,000 years before a team of paleontologists arrived to thaw him out. He is part man, part ape, and part fish, which accounts for his superior strength and not-so-pleasant odor.

Craig Kellman was asked to provide preliminary ideas for the shape and look of the monster. "Kellman's original drawings were really scary, so we asked him to draw a creature who didn't look like he was going to kill somebody," says art and modeling supervisor Jed Schlanger. "Craig gave us what we call the 'Bugs Bunny on a park bench pose,' and we all knew that was the one. From this drawing, we went straight to painting."

The idea was to create a combination fish/ape/man and visually discover the link among those three. Kellman modeled at least one of his designs on himself. "I wanted him to be the missing link from Cro-Magnon man and the fish that came out of the primordial ooze. He's a pre-ape man," says the artist. "I like the idea of a hairy ape fish because I have a lot of hair, so the character turns out to look a lot like me—which is, of course, sad for my wife!"

Kellman's original designs really struck a chord with the production team. "We had a character blitz moment with The Missing Link," says David James. "The character just came out and actually changed very little from these original conception drawings."

All of the characters go through a metamorphosis to uncover their personalities. Ideas are used, discarded, brought back, and sometimes discarded again. "The Missing Link is our most instinctive monster," explains Jed Schlanger, "He is the macho guy and, physically, the toughest monster in the movie."

Every monster has to have a specific relationship with Susan. For The Missing Link, he is the one monster who does not understand her at all. "At first, Link takes offense that Susan doesn't like being a monster," says Conrad Vernon. "That came off as him being a jerk, which we wanted to temper, so we put in more macho of him trying to impress her."

"The Missing Link likes the ladies and he's a little cheesy," says Vernon. "He used to grab women and throw them over his shoulder, because 20 million years ago that was perfectly acceptable. Women just don't buy that nowadays. The other problem is that when he throws women over his shoulder now, his back tends to go out on him. This idea was discovered in animation. We had an ad lib from Will Arnett, a grunt of pain, and animation tweaked his back. We discover a lot of physical comedy in animation."

(opposite) **Link Poster**—Timothy Lamb—digital paint. *(above)* **Link**—Timothy Lamb—digital paint.

(opposite and above) **Link**—Craig Kellman—digital paint.

We had a character blitz moment with The Missing Link. The character just came out and actually changed very little from these original conception drawings. The idea was to create a combination fish/ape/man and visually discover the link between those three.
—DAVID JAMES, PRODUCTION DESIGNER

(opposite and above) **Link**—Craig Kellman—pencil—Timothy Lamb—digital paint.

(above) **CG Still**. (below) **CG Still.** *(right)* **Link on the Prowl**—David James layout—

Timothy Lamb—digital paint.

B.O.B. is a good-natured but slightly lethargic gelatinous mass with an insatiable appetite. His powers include shape shifting, the ability to fit into any space, and the capacity to absorb anything.

How did B.O.B. come into being? He was created when a chemically modified ranch-flavored dessert topping was crossed with a genetically altered tomato at a snack food plant.

"If Dr. Cockroach is the brain and Link is the brawn, B.O.B. is the heart," says Lisa Stewart.

The design directive for B.O.B. could not have been more basic. He has one eye and a mouth; otherwise he is an amorphous lump. You would think that would make B.O.B. easy to design, but that was not the case.

The look of this hilarious character went through drastic transformations. "We had a B.O.B. task force because we had never created a character like this before," says David James.

"B.O.B. is a gelatinous mass, but he is a very real gelatinous mass," says art director Scott Wills. "You can see through him; you can see his interior bubbles. We wanted him to be as convincing as possible." Figuring out how to rig this character, make him move, and allow for him to be transparent without disappearing altogether was a real challenge for the filmmakers.

The actor Seth Rogen was hired to play the character, and added a sense of depth and emotion that was previously lacking. "Because of Seth, B.O.B. went from being dumb to being innocent with gumball thoughts that just come out of his mouth," says head of character animation David Burgess.

"Seth found the core of B.O.B.," agrees Lisa Stewart. "The character is not terribly bright but instead of playing him dumb, Seth infused him with this wide-eyed, childlike wonder. That, coupled with the wildly charming way he's animated, made B.O.B. a real scene stealer."

(opposite and above) **B.O.B. Poster**—Timothy Lamb—digital paint.

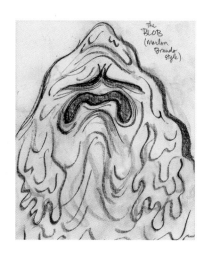

(above) **B.O.B.**—Craig Kellman—pencil. *(left)* **B.O.B.**—Craig Kellman & Devin Crane—character design—Timothy Lamb—digital paint. *(below)* **Early B.O.B.**—Peter Maynez—digital paint. *(right)* **B.O.B. in Cell**—Patrick Mate—character design—David James—layout—Michael Hernandez—digital paint. *(following pages)* **B.O.B.**—Timothy Lamb—digital paint.

(above) **B.O.B.**—Craig Kellman—pencil. (below and right) **B.O.B.**—JJ Villard—color pencil.

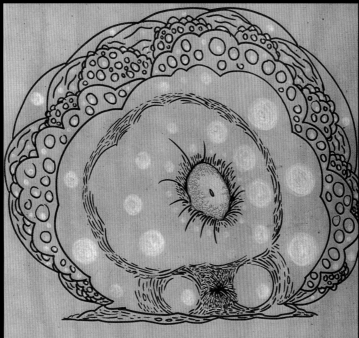
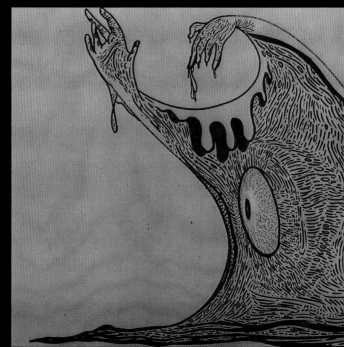

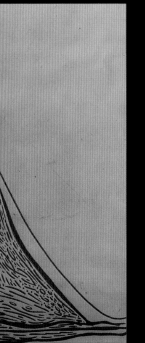
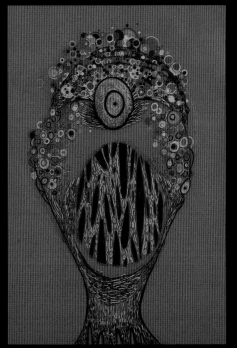
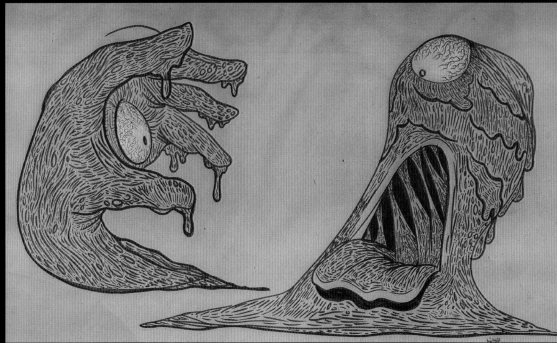

Insectosaurus was transformed from a grub into a misunderstood monster with a short temper by an unfortunate overdose of nuclear radiation. Since she can only express herself with screeches and chirps, she can't tell anyone that she's really a beautiful butterfly trapped in the body of a 350-foot grub. This inability to communicate and its inherent frustrations is the reason she once tried to destroy Tokyo.

Her powers include her super size, the ability to shoot sticky silk (Insectosaurus snot!) from her nostrils, and after she finally cocoons, the capacity to speak and fly at super speeds. Like a baby, she is attracted to and mesmerized by bright lights.

"Early on, we decided Insectosaurus was incredibly fat and had no mobility," says Craig Kellman, character designer. "We gave her tiny arms with this huge, huge body. Her limited motion is a funny character trait."

While Dr. Cockroach and B.O.B. were relatively simple in their basic design, Insectosaurus was difficult to conceive. "Other than getting Susan right, the biggest design challenge was Insectosaurus," admits David James. "From a design perspective, her pendulum swung from grotesque to cutesy. We wanted a certain amount of grossness that turned out to be frankly distasteful."

Finding the balance for a character that is supposed to be gross yet endearing isn't easy. Ultimately, the problem boiled down to Insectosaurus's enormous puffy lips, which seemed to offend almost everyone. Once the lips were shrunk and softened, the look for Insectosaurus was finalized.

For all of the characters in the movie, other than the humans, the surfacing waivered between realistic and cartoony, although Insectosaurus represented the most cartoon-like character of all. "Insectosaurus has realistic scales but most of her surfacing and color has a more cartoony feel," explains Scott Wills. "To me she looks like a big toy."

Toy or not, Insectosaurus was created to be loveable. "The final design still retained its fun, big-baby-bug, gross-out integrity, but wasn't so much over the top," says James. "In the end, she turned out to be a cross between a big baby and a Golden Retriever. She's loyal and innocent, but not really intelligible."

INSECTOSAURUS

(opposite) **Insecto Poster**—Timothy Lamb—digital paint. *(above right and right)* **Insecto**—Craig Kellman—color pencil.

Insectosaurus has realistic scales but most of her surfacing and color has a cartoony feel.
—SCOTT WILLS, ART DIRECTOR

(above left) **Insecto**—Craig Kellman—character design—Timothy Lamb—digital paint. *(above right)* **Insecto**—Craig Kellman—pencil.

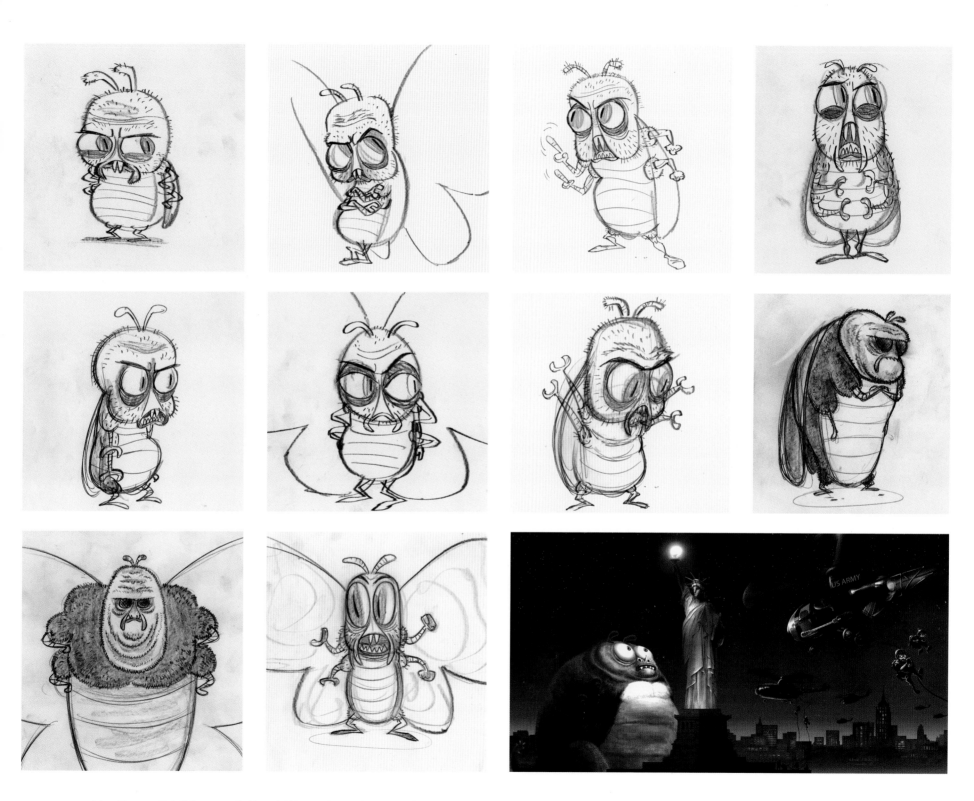

(above) **Insecto**—Craig Kellman—pencil. (above right) **Insecto Capture Concept**—Patrick Hanenberger—digital paint & character design.

(left) **Insecto Underwater**—Ronald Kurniawan—Digital Paint.
(above and right) **Insecto Transformed**—Timothy Lamb—digital paint. (below) **Insecto Transformed 2**—Timothy Lamb—pencil.

GALLAXHAR

For many reasons, Gallaxhar was another problematic character to create. Because there were no limitations on who or what the villain could be, there were also no limitations on what he (or she) could look like.

At first, the filmmakers wanted a female villain because they had a female heroine; there was some inherent symmetry to having two females square off against each other. Then they considered modeling Gallaxhar after a Texas oil baron. At various times, he/she was an intergalactic oil baron, a three-eyed, multi-limbed cat, a head in a lava lamp, and an elephant scorpion.

"We sent Craig Kellman off and said we wanted a little bit of the 1950s space alien but we needed a new element, something that says 1950s space alien without saying *typical* 1950s space alien," says Conrad Vernon.

Kellman pictured Gallaxhar as heartless and very politically incorrect. "Originally he was the ultimate consumer, gas guzzler, and resource waster," says Kellman. "A total sloth with no concern for the environment." In other words, the quintessential bad guy for the twenty-first century.

"Craig's mind works in fifty different directions at once, so he came in with crazy, hilarious, and scary concepts," explains Vernon. "We chose the elements we liked and sent him back to work. He returned with another version and we had it."

Like Insectosaurus, here was another huge balancing act between gross and ridiculous, but with a third ingredient: ultimately threatening and evil. "The final Gallaxhar design reflects those three parts coming together to make a ludicrously caricatured space octopus with a hydrocephalic condition who is also an arch villain," explains David James.

Another balancing act in terms of the character was that Gallaxhar had to be both menacing and humorous at the same time. "The

(above) **Gallaxhar Explorations**—Craig Kellman—digital paint. *(opposite)* **Gallaxhar Explorations**—Craig Kellman—character design—Timothy Lamb—digital paint.

(opposite, far right) **Gallaxhar**—Craig Kellman—character design—Timothy Lamb—digital paint.

menace part came from giving him a clear rationale and a clear plan," says head of story Peter Ramsey. "In trying to keep the story simple, we opted for a classic alien invasion with the twist that he is so megalomaniacal he wants to populate the Earth with his clones. The original impetus for that came from Derek, Susan's fiancé, who has megalomaniacal tendencies at the start of the film. The idea is supposed to be that, in the end, Susan defeats Gallaxhar because she's dealt with this kind of guy before."

Like all the characters in the movie, Gallaxhar evolved during production. "We discovered things about that character as we went along that we didn't know at the beginning," explains Vernon. "We knew his plot and we knew his plan. We knew what he wanted to do and how he wanted to do it, but we didn't know who he was. From Craig's design, because of how the character looked, we could start visualizing his surroundings and who he was."

The art of the final character is insanely exaggerated with his huge head, long tentacles, short arms, tiny antennas, arched eyebrows, and Salvador Dali mustache. He has a scary-looking face with a perpetually malevolent grimace, and although he is both villainous and evil, he also retains an element of humor with his blue and purple striped skin and mod disco shirt.

"Rainn (Wilson) came in to do the voice, and really started to tell us who Gallaxhar was," says Vernon. "The artists and then the animators added a lot to the character. Gallaxhar is truly a collaboration."

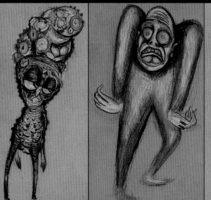

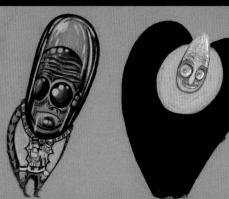

(above) **Early Gallaxhar**—Devin Crane—digital paint.
(right) **Gallaxhar Explorations**—JJ Villard—color pencil. *(following pages)* **Gallaxhar's Bridge**—Timothy Lamb—digital paint—Ritche Sacilioc—3D design.

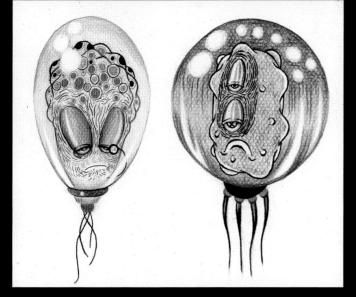

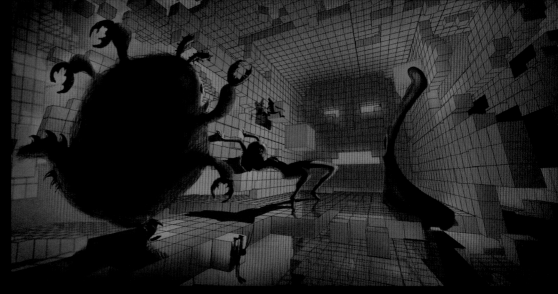

(above left) **Gallaxhar Explorations**—JJ Villard—color pencil. *(above right)* **Digital Gallaxhar**—Patrick Mate—character design—Patrick Hanenberger—digital paint.

(below left) **Digital Gallaxhar**—Patrick Hanenberger—digital paint. *(below right)* **Digital Gallaxhar With Robot**—Patrick Hanenberger—digital paint.

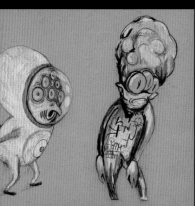

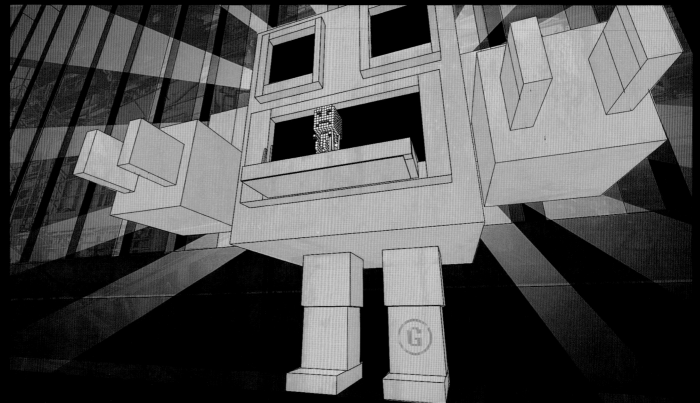

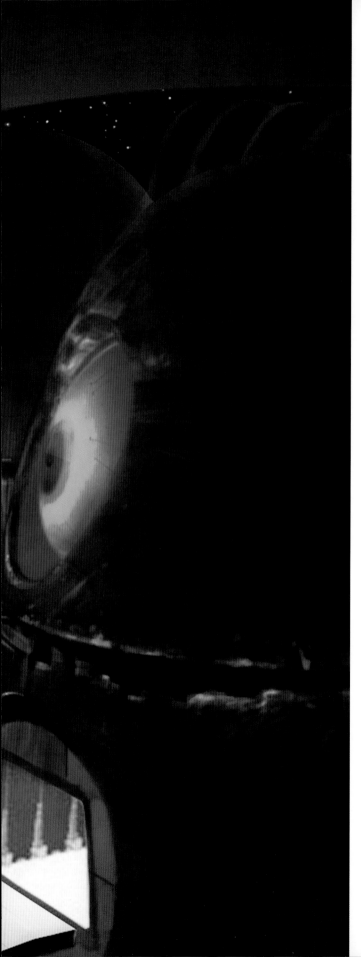

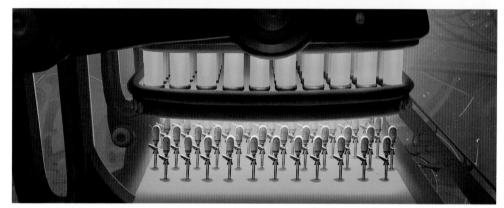

GALLAXHAR'S CLONES

The ultimate megalomaniac, Gallaxhar is determined to clone himself over and over so that he can populate the planet with mini-versions of himself. The clones provide many opportunities for humor. "Here was a huge opportunity for comedy with the megalomaniac twist," says Peter Ramsey. "The stuff that worked the best for me with Gallaxhar deals with the clones. We have hundreds of thousands of copies of the same person. Each one thinks he is in charge."

> The idea that Gallaxhar clones himself made us rethink the way the story played. We always try to find the signpost thing about a character and flesh that out.
> —PETER RAMSEY, HEAD OF STORY

(left) **The Hangar**—Richard Daskas—digital paint—Patrick Hanenberger—3D design. *(above top)* **Cloner**—Timothy Lamb—digital paint—Peter Maynez—3D design. *(above)* **Cloner Stamp**—Chris Brock—digital paint—Peter Maynez—3D design.

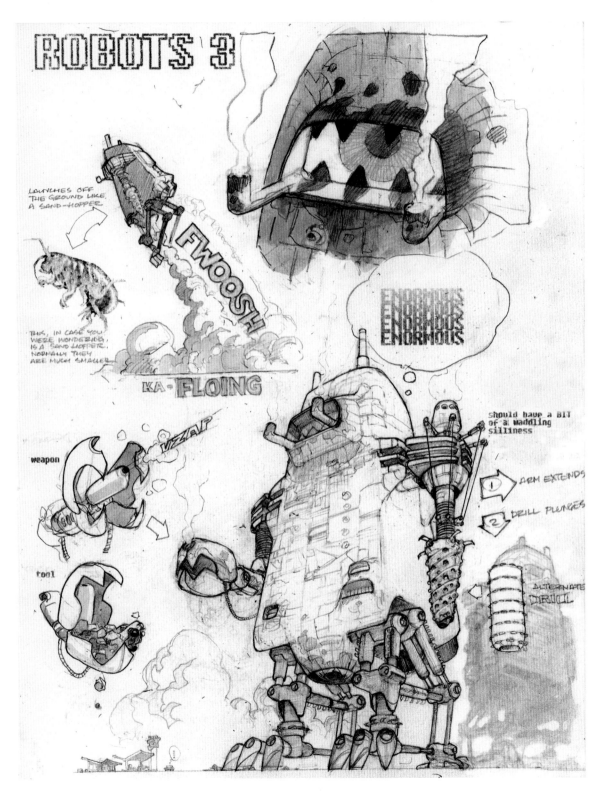

ROBOTS

Gallaxhar's robots are programmed to find and process energy resources (oil, minerals, coal, plutonium, quantonium) throughout the universe.

The robots are so massive that they can hold thousands of smaller robots. The design underwent many changes from very complicated insect-like beings to a simple round shape that seemed more in keeping with the alien shape language established in the movie. Basically, they are walking oilrigs with a brain and an eye. They can walk, roll, drill, dig, grab, shoot out flames, scan the environment with lasers, and gather materials. They are very compact working machines with a multitude of skills and functions.

The robot enters the atmosphere in the form of a capsule but, once active, it unfolds itself into a humanoid walking factory. To return to the Mothership, the robot folds itself back into capsule form.

The basic design approach for the robot was to keep the large movements and silhouette simple so that, from a distance, there is minimal movement. Up close, however, there is a lot more detail in the inner workings. Inside the robot are lots of gears spinning, tubes stretching, and hydraulics pumping.

(above) **Robot Exploration**—David James—pencil & digital paint. *(opposite)* **Robot Exploration**—Patrick Hanenberger—digital paint.

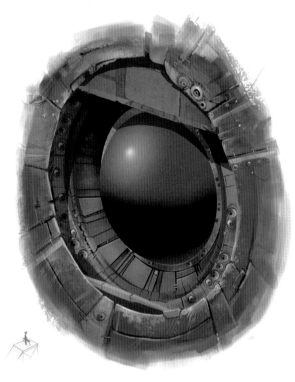

(*above*) **Robo Eye**—Patrick Hanenberger—digital paint.

(*right*) **Robot**—Patrick Hanenberger—digital paint.

The robots are the landing ships, the utility knives of Gallaxhar's industrial machinery. They can go down to Earth, mine for resources, explore, and transport.

—PATRICK HANENBERGER, VISUAL DEVELOPMENT ARTIST

(above) **Robot Explorations**—Patrick Hanenberger—pencil & digital paint. (below) **Robot Arm**—
Patrick Hanenberger—pencil & digital paint. (below right) **Robot Hand**—Peter Maynez—pen & marker.
(following pages) **Robot First Contact**—Patrick Hanenberger—digital paint.

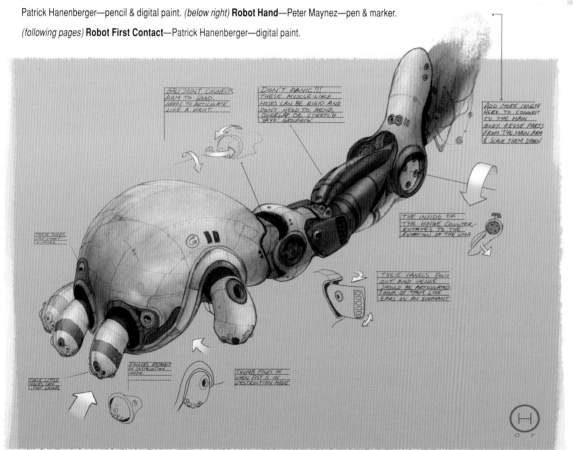

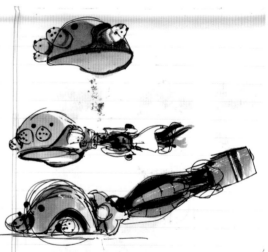

ROBOT ARM WHICH EXTENDS FROM ROBOT SHAPE
IT'S ALMOST LIKE A FRIENDLY SHAPE, LIKE!

PRESIDENT HATHAWAY

As mentioned, "First Contact" and "The War Room" were the first two scenes written for the movie. "Mike Mitchell and I just started throwing out gags which Mike then boarded," says Conrad Vernon. "These storyboards set the tone for the character of the president. He is the goofiest character in the War Room. Everyone takes him totally seriously and never acknowledges how ridiculous he is."

Much of the look for the character was inspired by the work of artist Jack Davis of *Mad* magazine. "To me, the design and character conceit of this movie is Ed Wood meets *Mad* magazine," says head of character animation David Burgess. "Our president definitely has a

(above left) **Presidential Portrait**—Ronald Kurniawan—digital paint. *(above right)* **Presidential Portrait**—Ronald Kurniawan—pencil & digital paint.

Mad magazine aesthetic, with his big ears and stylized hair. His proportions are by no means human. Realistic human proportions are 6½ to 7 heads tall. This means that if you took the size of your head and multiplied it by 6½ to 7, you'd get your height. We made the president about 4 heads tall. We've pushed his design and proportions like that to get a stylized animation and find a unique style for him."

Oversized floppy hands were added as another key characteristic of the president that gave him an added cartoony feel.

The character is given voice by Stephen Colbert, who coincidentally bears an uncanny resemblance to the character (the president was drawn long before Colbert was cast for the part).

During his recording sessions, Colbert embraced the character and added dimension and humor to the character. "Stephen Colbert might be the most quick-witted person I've ever met," notes producer Lisa Stewart.

(above) **President Golfing**—Patrick Hanenberger—digital paint—David James—layout—Patrick Mate—character design. *(above center)* **President Explorations**—Craig Kellman—pencil.

(above right) **President**—Devin Crane—character design—Timothy Lamb—digital paint. *(following pages)* **President & General**—Craig Kellman—character design—Richard Daskas—digital paint.

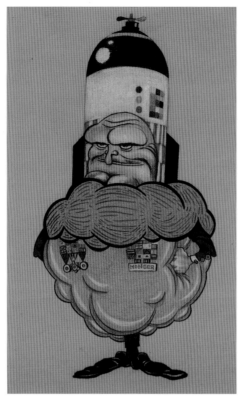

GENERAL W. R. MONGER AND OTHER HUMANS

Chief among the supporting cast of players in the movie is General W. R. Monger, a career military man, the prototype from many war movies. He could be described as a cross between George C. Scott in *Doctor Strangelove* and Lee Marvin in *The Dirty Dozen*. Played with great fervor by Kiefer Sutherland, Monger runs Area Fifty-Something, where the captured monsters are being held. Monger has the president's ear on all things military.

Derek, Susan's fiancé, is a weatherman in Modesto, California, and perfectly happy to marry Susan until she grows to 49 feet, 11 inches. Then he immediately breaks off their engagement. Paul Rudd plays Derek and was instrumental in defining the character, particularly in his break-up scene with Susan. "It was difficult to find the proper tone for this scene," says Lisa Stewart. "We didn't want Derek to simply be a jerk, nor did we want Susan to be a doormat. So we brought Reese and Paul in to record together and let them play around with different approaches. Paul settled on this befuddled Ted Knight kind of guy and really helped set the tone."

Other humans in supporting roles were Susan's parents and other members of the bridal party, as well as all the military personnel.

For group and crowd scenes, designers created generic heads and dispersed them throughout the background. This is a common practice in animated features when the background of a scene needs to be filled with characters. Instead of creating individual people, a few prototypes are created and then duplicated to fill whatever space needs filling.

(above) **General Monger Explorations**—JJ Villard—color pencil.

74

(above) **General Monger**—Craig Kellman—pencil. *(below and far right)* **General Monger**—Chris Reccardi—pencil. *(right)* **General Monger**—Timothy Lamb—digital paint—Devin Crane—character design.

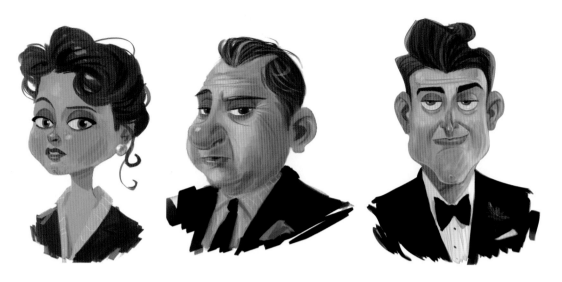

(above left) **Ms. Ronson**—Devin Crane—digital paint. (above center) **Carl Murphy**—Devin Crane—digital paint. (above right) **Derek**—Devin Crane—digital paint. (below left) **Katie and Cuthbert**—Devin Crane—digital paint. (below center) **Rita Dietl**—Devin Crane—digital paint. (below right) **Bridesmaids**—Devin Crane—digital paint.

(above left) **War Room Advisors**—Devin Crane—digital paint. *(above right)* **Generic Kids**—Devin Crane—pencil & digital paint. *(below)* **Generic Women**—Devin Crane—pencil & digital paint.

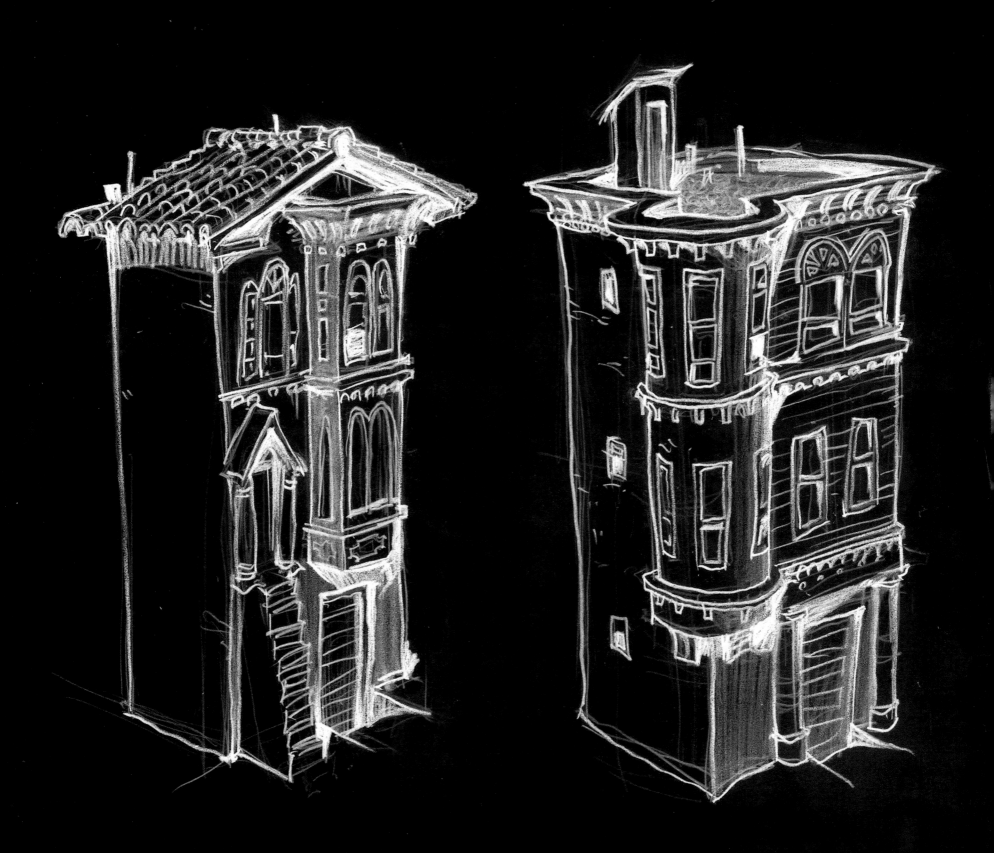

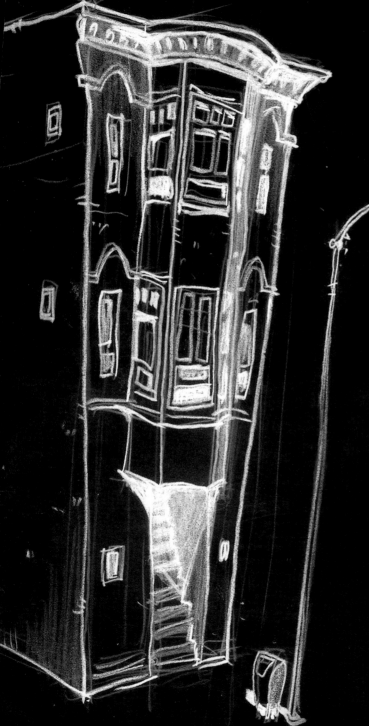

PART TWO

LOCATIONS

MODESTO, CALIFORNIA

Susan's home is in Modesto, California, a place meant to exemplify rural small-town America. "The architecture and landscape here help define Susan as a small-town girl wondering about the big world out there," says art director Michael Isaak. "Susan has to grow away from Derek. The story needed small-town imagery to hit home and help define her character."

Originally, the art department created an entire city including shops and a movie theater. In the end, though, these locations were pared down considerably. "We designed the entire town but ended up using only four locations," says Michael Isaak.

First, there is the church where Susan is about to marry Derek. This place represented the promise of Susan's life. The church is so small that Susan literally busts through the ceiling.

The second location, Susan's family home, represented her most comfortable place so it was designed in warm colors to be friendly and welcoming.

"Derek's news station was kind of pathetic looking, like Derek himself," says Isaak. "This place represents the far reaches of the dial, one step up from cable news access. We wanted to show that Susan's life with Derek would be small and limited."

Finally, there is the gas station, where Susan is at her absolute lowest point in the story and this is emphasized by her surroundings. The station seems to be in the middle of nowhere, on a long forgotten highway that time has passed by. The place was meant to feel as lonely and desolate as Susan feels at this point.

Whether the location looked realistic or cartoony, these four locations were created to emphasize whatever was happening in the scene. "Each of these places was pushed in a unique way according to what was needed for the scene," says Isaak.

(previous pages) **San Francisco Buildings**—Timothy Lamb—pencil. *(above)* **Downtown Modesto**—Rachel Tiep-Daniels—3D design

(left) **Susan's House**—Timothy Lamb—digital paint—Rachel Tiep-Daniels—3D design.

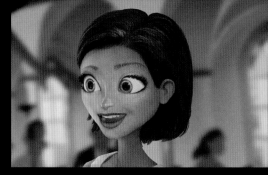

(above) **Susan Glowing**—Richard Daskas—digital paint.
(above left) **The Wedding**—Richard Daskas—digital paint—Rachel Tiep-Daniels—3D design. *(left)* **Wedding Day**—Chris Brock—digital paint—Rachel Tiep-Daniels—3D design. *(below)* **Suasn Grows**—Tim Lamb—digital paint. *(opposite above)* **Susan Breaks Out**—Chris Brock—digital paint. *(opposite below)* **News Station**—Chris Brock—digital paint.

FIRST CONTACT

The so-called "First Contact" location is the place where the aliens land in the United States, the "only country UFO's ever seem to land in," as a reporter remarks in the film.

Where exactly on American soil does First Contact take place? That is a hard question to answer. During production, the exact location moved frequently. For a long time, the initial site was in Texas, but then it moved around the Midwest for a period. In the script it was identified as Yuma, Arizona, for a while before finally turning into California.

Now this location is a generic town somewhere on the coast of California, a town with orange groves, lots of agriculture, and a place known as Make-out Point, although surely every town in America boasts a Make-out Point.

The aliens land at Make-out Point during the night but it takes some time before the military realizes they've arrived, so the scene where the President meets the aliens happens right at sunrise. This was perfect timing because the look for the scene was fashioned after a quintessential war movie. "My first idea was to create a kind of *Apocalypse Now* morning shot with the helicopters flying in at dawn," explains art director Scott Wills. "We wanted to appeal to everyone and to be dramatic but not get carried away. This was our starting off point and though we pulled back, the scene still retains some of that feeling. It is pretty goofy, I'll admit."

(top) **Lubbock Make-out Point**—Ronald Kurniawan—digital paint. *(above center)* **Make-out Blast**—Ritche Sacilioc—digital paint.
(above) **Make Out**—Ritche Sacilioc—digital paint. *(opposite)* **Katie and Cuthbert**—Richard Daskas—digital paint.

(all) **First Contact Color Keys**—Scott Wills, Timothy Lamb—digital paint.

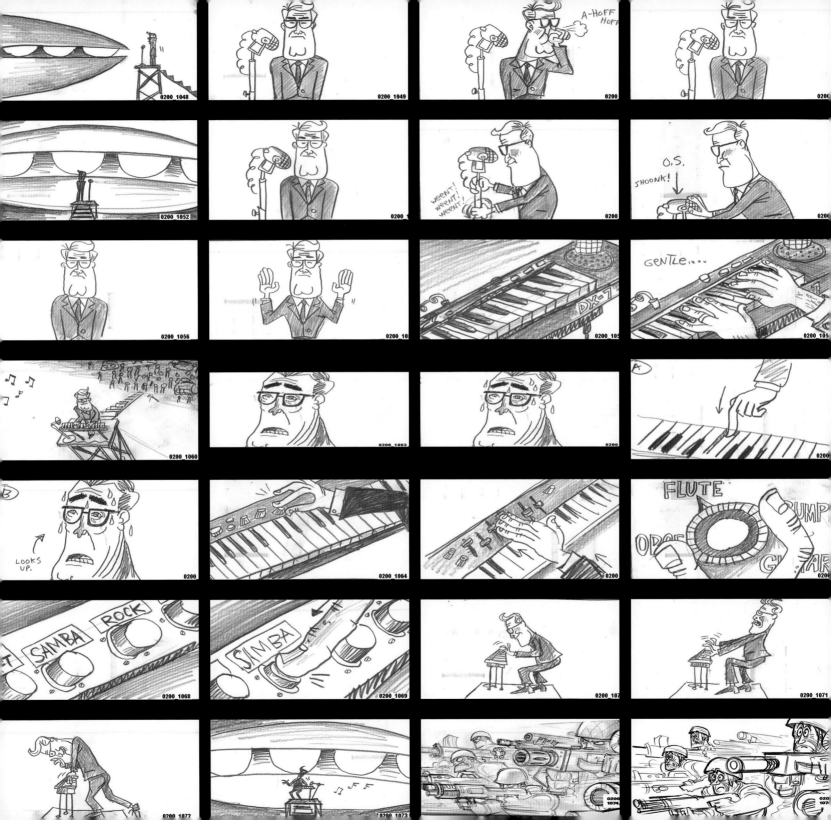

(*all*) **CG stills**.

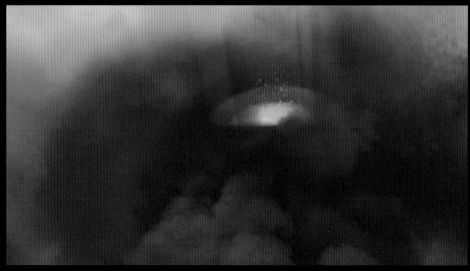

AREA FIFTY-SOMETHING

Once Susan is tranquilized and abducted by the government, she is brought to this undisclosed area. There is a running joke in the movie that anyone who utters the name of this place gets immediately darted and whisked away.

The exterior of Area Fifty-Something has a bleak and forlorn look, a cross between the red rock canyons of Utah and the surface of the moon. (Though this image is no longer in the movie, it helps to show the tone of the location and the thinking behind its inception.) The inside, or perhaps it's more accurate to say "underneath," Area Fifty-Something is the Monster Prison, and this is where Susan is taken. She awakes the morning after her abduction to find herself ensconced in a holding cell. Here she will meet her fellow monsters.

(opposite) **Area-ssh!**—David James—digital paint. *(top)* **Lobby**—Richard Daskas—digital paint. *(above)* **Area-ssh!**—color concepts—Patrick Hanenberger—digital paint.

93

(above) **Interior Cavern**—Ritche Sacilioc—3D design & digital paint. (below) **Monster Capture Squad**—Michael Isaak—pencil & digital paint.

(opposite) **Area Cross Section Map**—Kevin Conran—digital paint.

Kevin Conran's Cross Section Map clearly sets the tone for the movie by mixing the silliness of fun gags with the architecture of a believable structure. Our designers and story people used this early drawing as a launching pad of ideas.

—MICHAEL ISAAK, ART DIRECTOR

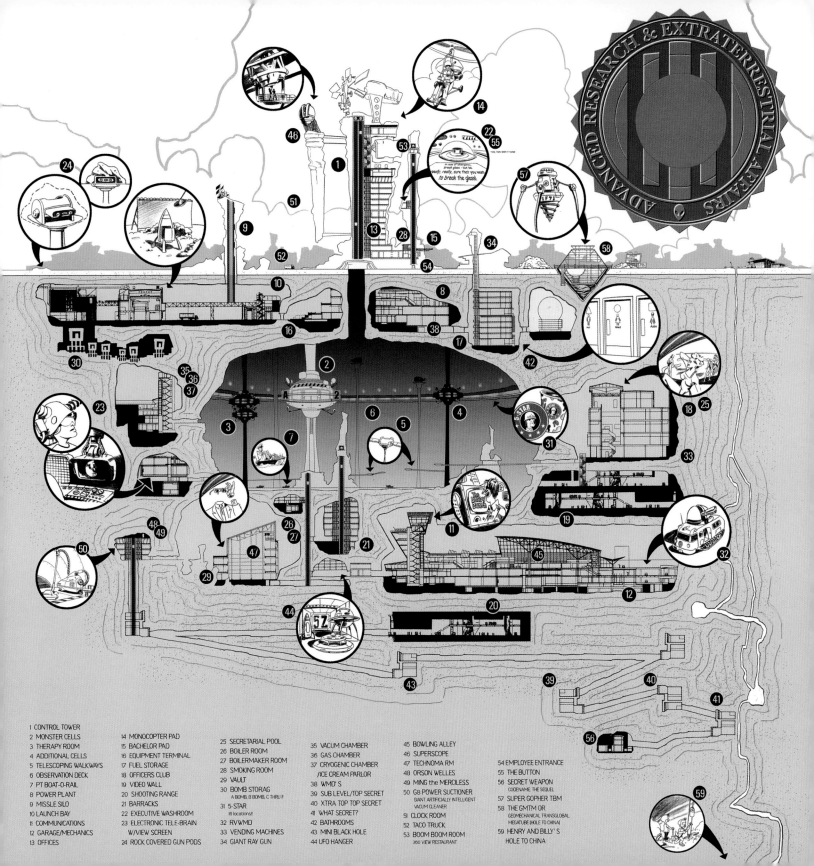

ADVANCED RESEARCH & EXTRATERRESTRIAL AFFAIRS

1 CONTROL TOWER
2 MONSTER CELLS
3 THERAPY ROOM
4 ADDITIONAL CELLS
5 TELESCOPING WALKWAYS
6 OBSERVATION DECK
7 PT BOAT-O-RAIL
8 POWER PLANT
9 MISSLE SILO
10 LAUNCH BAY
11 COMMUNICATIONS
12 GARAGE/MECHANICS
13 OFFICES

14 MONOCOPTER PAD
15 BACHELOR PAD
16 EQUIPMENT TERMINAL
17 FUEL STORAGE
18 OFFICERS CLUB
19 VIDEO WALL
20 SHOOTING RANGE
21 BARRACKS
22 EXECUTIVE WASHROOM
23 ELECTRONIC TELE-BRAIN
   W/VIEW SCREEN
24 ROCK COVERED GUN PODS

25 SECRETARIAL POOL
26 BOILER ROOM
27 BOILERMAKER ROOM
28 SMOKING ROOM
29 VAULT
30 BOMB STORAG
   A BOMB, B BOMB, C THRU F
31 5-STAR
   16 locations!
32 RVWMD
33 VENDING MACHINES
34 GIANT RAY GUN

35 VACUM CHAMBER
36 GAS CHAMBER
37 CRYOGENIC CHAMBER
   /ICE CREAM PARLOR
38 WMD'S
39 SUB LEVEL/TOP SECRET
40 XTRA TOP TOP SECRET
41 WHAT SECRET?
42 BATHROOMS
43 MINI BLACK HOLE
44 UFO HANGER

45 BOWLING ALLEY
46 SUPERSCOPE
47 TECHNOMA RM
48 ORSON WELLES
49 MING the MERCILESS
50 G8 POWER SUCTIONER
   GIANT ARTIFICIALLY INTELLIGENT
   VACUM CLEANER
51 CLOCK ROOM
52 TACO TRUCK
53 BOOM BOOM ROOM
   360 VIEW RESTAURANT

54 EMPLOYEE ENTRANCE
55 THE BUTTON
56 SECRET WEAPON
   CODENAME: THE SEQUEL
57 SUPER GOPHER TBM
58 THE GMTM OR
   GEOMECHANICAL TRANSGLOBAL
   MEGATUBE (HOLE TO CHINA)
59 HENRY AND BILLY'S
   HOLE TO CHINA

MONSTER PRISON

DreamWorks Animation art director Michael Isaak has a degree in architecture, an education that came in handy when he was assigned the task of art directing the prison where the monsters would be housed at the beginning of our story. Isaak thought long and hard about solving the problem of warehousing monsters. "The biggest and most fun challenge was trying to think like a paranoid government official in the 1950s," explains Isaak, with glee. "If the government really believed there was a monster problem, and they were terrified, what would they do? I figured they'd overbuild, of course! If they caught five monsters, they'd think this was only the tip of the iceberg and they'd be capturing a monster a day for the next hundred years. So they'd build a prison to house thousands of monsters. This adds to the humor because we have one small group of *One Flew Over the Cookoo's*

Nest misfits in this gigantically over-designed space." (See image on page 95.)

The design concept for the building is simple, especially compared to the lavishly detailed Mothership. Basically, the prison is a geometrical cylinder. "It's like a pole stuck in the ground," says Isaak. All of the various rooms work off this shape.

Inside, the prison boasts an elaborate transport system. "I figured there'd be an insane amount of stuff needed to feed and house these monsters so we created a crate system where pads lock in to transport food and equipment," explains Isaak. "The transport system was designed to keep human and monster contact completely separate; they never interact. The monsters have an internal elevator system while the humans use an external one."

Though the transport system is not really

(opposite) **Area Commisary**—Chris Brock—digital paint—Michael Isaak—3D Design.

(above) **Area Hallway**—David James—pen & marker storyboard.

color variations

featured in the film, like many other details, it was nonetheless crafted to perfection. "We don't want to draw too much attention to it," Isaak admits, "but we wanted to make sure that it looked like it really worked."

The overall appearance of the prison is cold and sterile, with an eerie bluish cast from fluorescent lights. All the colors inside the prison are deliberately muted. By muting the background, the colors of the monsters showcase their vibrant personalities: the bright blue of luminous B.O.B., the greens of The Missing Link, the orange-reds of Dr. Cockroach, the purple hues of Insectosaurus, and Susan with her platinum-white hair and orange jumpsuit. These colors pop off the screen when set against the sterile walls of the prison.

The cumulative effect of these design decisions is to create a monster prison that comes off as a very mysterious, unknown, and bizarre place for both Susan and the audience.

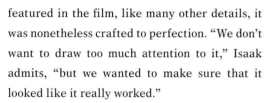

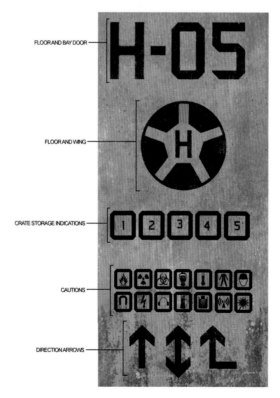

FLOOR AND BAY DOOR

FLOOR AND WING

CRATE STORAGE INDICATIONS

CAUTIONS

DIRECTION ARROWS

(above left) **Area Transport Crates**—Michael Isaak—digital paint. *(above)* **Hallway**—Ronald Kurniawan—digital paint—Michael Isaak—3D design. *(left)* **Area Graphics**—Michael Isaak—digital paint. *(opposite right)* **Insecto Cell**—Michael Isaak, Brett Nystul—3D design—Ronald Kurniawan—digital paint. *(opposite left)* **Susan's Cell**—Brett Nystul—3D design—Chris Brock—digital paint.

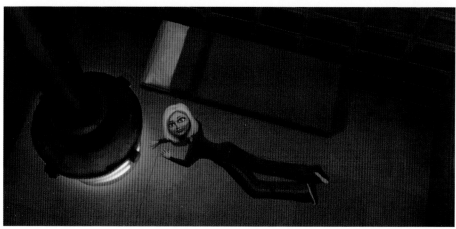

(*above*) **Hallway Key**—Ronald Kurnlawan—digital paint—Michael Isaak—3D design. (*below left*) **Insecto's Cell Key**—Ronald Kurniawan—digital paint—Michael Isaak—3D design.

(*below right*) **Link's Cell Key**—Chris Brock—digital paint. (*opposite*) **External Cylinder Key**—Richard Daskas—digital paint—Michael Isaak—3D design.

THE WAR ROOM

During the course of production, the War Room underwent a drastic transformation. At first, it was conceived and designed as a kind of party room for the amusement of a not-too-studious president. "The original idea was that the president designed the War Room himself," says Michael Isaak. "Though he's running the country, that is not his top priority and he's not very good at it. It's his idea that with the flick of a switch, the War Room changes into a kind of Playboy party lounge with a pool table and buffet bars. The president can't wait for the party to begin."

The idea was a lot of fun and allowed for all kinds of visual jokes, but it fell by the wayside because it proved to be a little too goofy for the story. David James describes it as a "hat on a hat" joke, meaning there were so many jokes going on in the room that they canceled each other out.

"The two-button joke [one red button for latte, one for nuclear attack] is the retained joke from that sequence," explains James. "But for that joke to work, it had to be in the context of a serious environment or else you wouldn't buy it. If the entire place was goofy, there was no potential for surprise. If you are expecting a joke,

(above) **Early War Room Lounge**—Richard Daskas—digital paint. *(opposite)* **Early War Room**—Richard Daskas—digital paint.

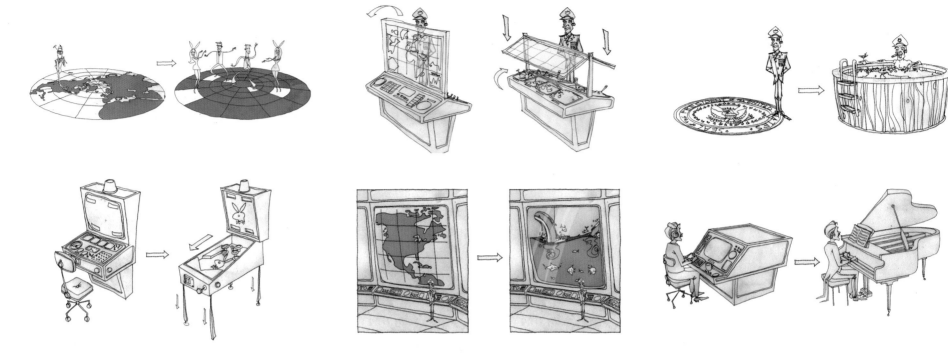

it fails. The world needs to be the straight man to the absurdity."

Once the decision was made to keep the setting serious and the dialogue funny, the designers needed to create a more traditional look for the War Room. "In our collective unconsciousness, we all have an idea about the look of a War Room," says Isaak. "Even though it does not exist, we've seen it in so many films, we think we know what it looks like. We didn't want to spoof that idea; we wanted to play that straight."

In the end the War Room is very business-like, but not without a sense of humor. Would a real War Room include an Elbow and Butt Scanner?

(above) **War Room Transforms Into Lounge**—Michael Isaak— pencil & digital paint. (right) **Still**.

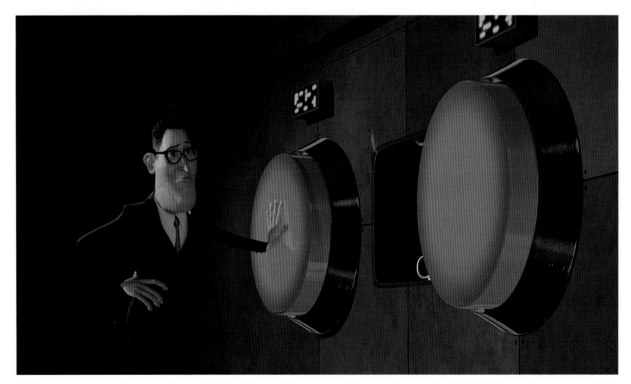

(above) **War Room Key**—Scott Wills—digital paint—Michael Isaak—layout & character design. (below) **War Room Models**—Michael Isaak—3D design.

(above) **Military Uniforms**—Ronald Kurniawan—digital paint.

(left) **Defense Insignia**—Ronald Kurniawan—digital paint.

(below) **Medals**—Ronald Kurniawan—digital paint.

(right) **War Room**—Richard Daskas—digital paint.

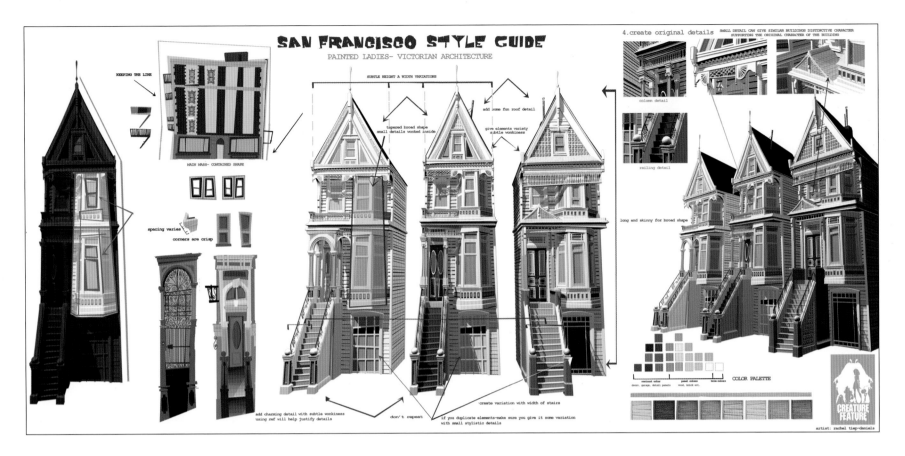

SAN FRANCISCO

San Francisco is the location for the first major action/chase sequence in the movie. This is a complicated sequence.

"For the San Francisco location, our intention was not to be accurate for the residents of the city, but to get the flavor of the city across to the audience," explains Michael Isaak. "To this end, we studied things like the style of the buildings, the setbacks, the relationship of the trees to the power lines, and such. These things leave a collective unconscious visual memory of the city. San Francisco is defined by such images as its Victorian architecture, the hills, the water, the harbor, the Golden Gate Bridge,

the Transamerica building, and even the fog. With these kinds of details in mind, we can re-create the flavor of the city."

The climactic moment in San Francisco is the destruction of the Golden Gate Bridge. During the course of the action, the cables of the bridge snap off, a giant robot uses his grinding innards to slice through and then crack a huge hole in the bridge. The Golden Gate Bridge is split in half when Insectosaurus and the giant robot square off. And eventually the entire bridge collapses.

Visual development artist Rachel Tiep-Daniels was responsible for drawing architectural and engineering plans for the bridge so that when parts of it broke off, the structural aspect

of its destruction would be absolutely accurate. "We did push some of the shapes to give the bridge something of a cartoony feel," explains Michael Isaak. "The top of the bridge flares out and the proportions and lines have something of a traditional cartoon sense, but it is important to give the audience a sense of peril. We had to make the bridge feel real and make it understandable that the people in those cars could really get hurt. On the other hand, some comic elements were added to make it not so scary." The art of the scene was to make it look and feel both perilous and humorous, which is a very delicate balance, and one that was characteristic of so many scenes in the movie.

(above) **San Francisco Style Guide**—Rachel Tiep Daniels—3D design & digital paint.

(top left) **Building Study**—Timothy Lamb—pencil. *(above)* **San Francisco Visual Development**—Timothy Lamb—pencil. *(above right)* **Building Paintings**—Rachel Tiep-Daniels—digital paint

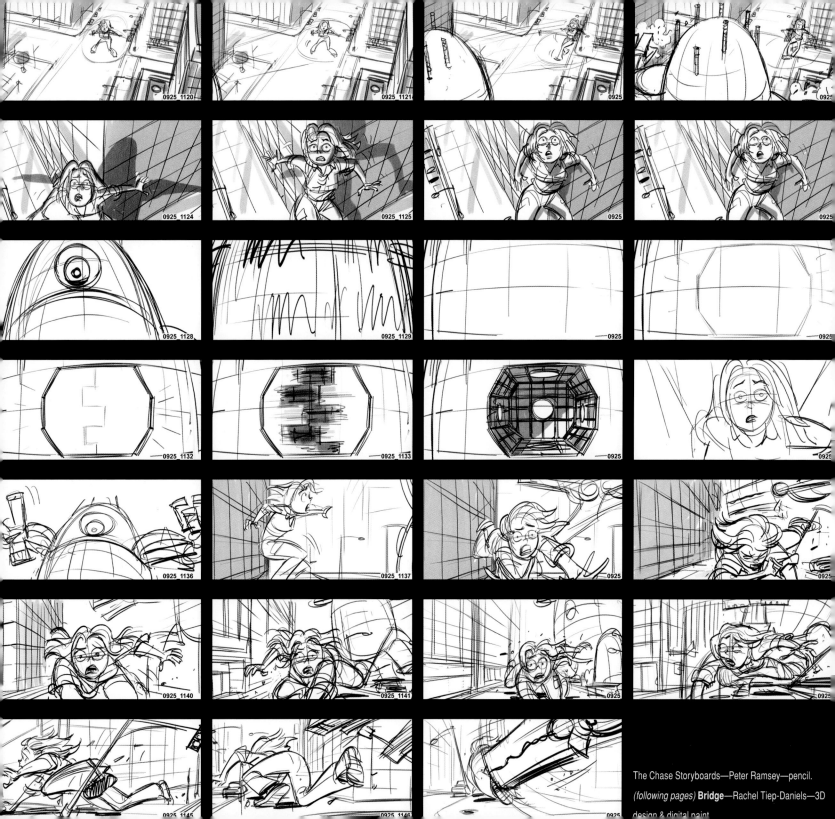

The Chase Storyboards—Peter Ramsey—pencil.

(following pages) Bridge—Rachel Tiep-Daniels—3D
design & digital paint

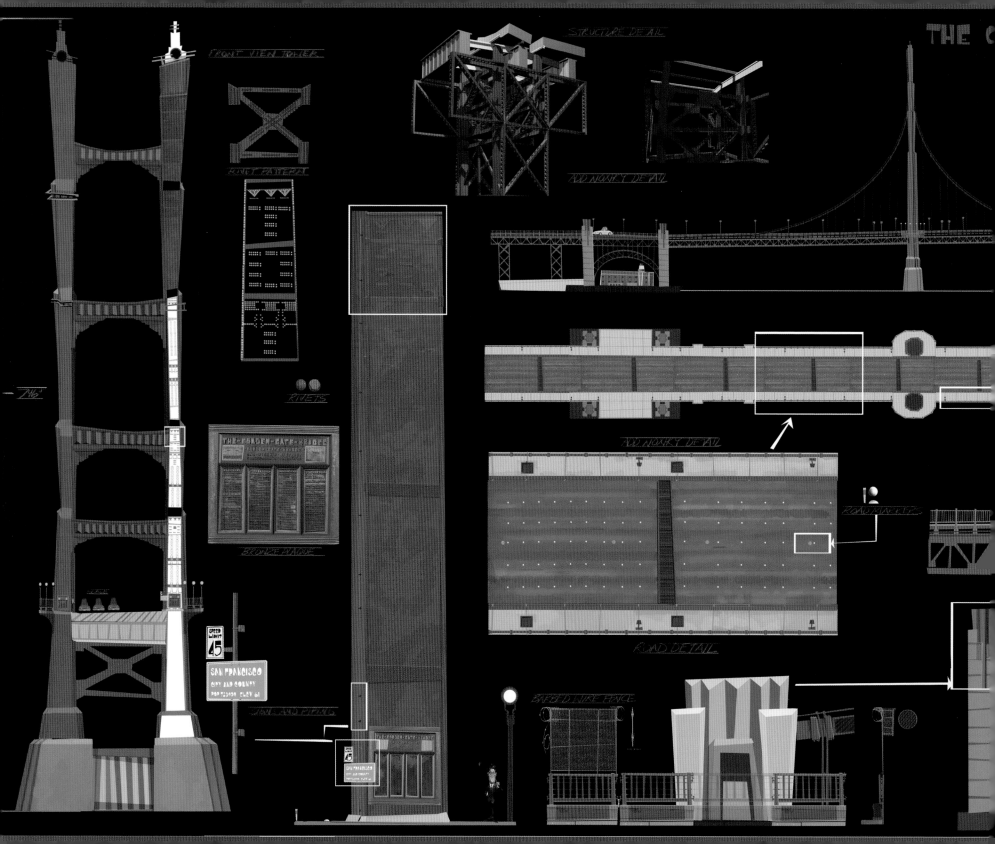

FRONT VIEW TOWER

STRUCTURE DETAIL

THE G

RIVET PATTERN

ADD NOXRY DETAIL

RIVETS

THE GOLDEN GATE BRIDGE

ADD NOXRY DETAIL

ROAD MARKERS

BRONZE PLAQUE

ROAD DETAIL

SPEED LIMIT 45

SAN FRANCISCO
CITY AND COUNTY
POP 733450 ELEV 61

LANE AND PAPERS

BARBED WIRE FENCE

SPEED LIMIT 45

SAN FRANCISCO
CITY AND COUNTY
POP 733450 ELEV 61

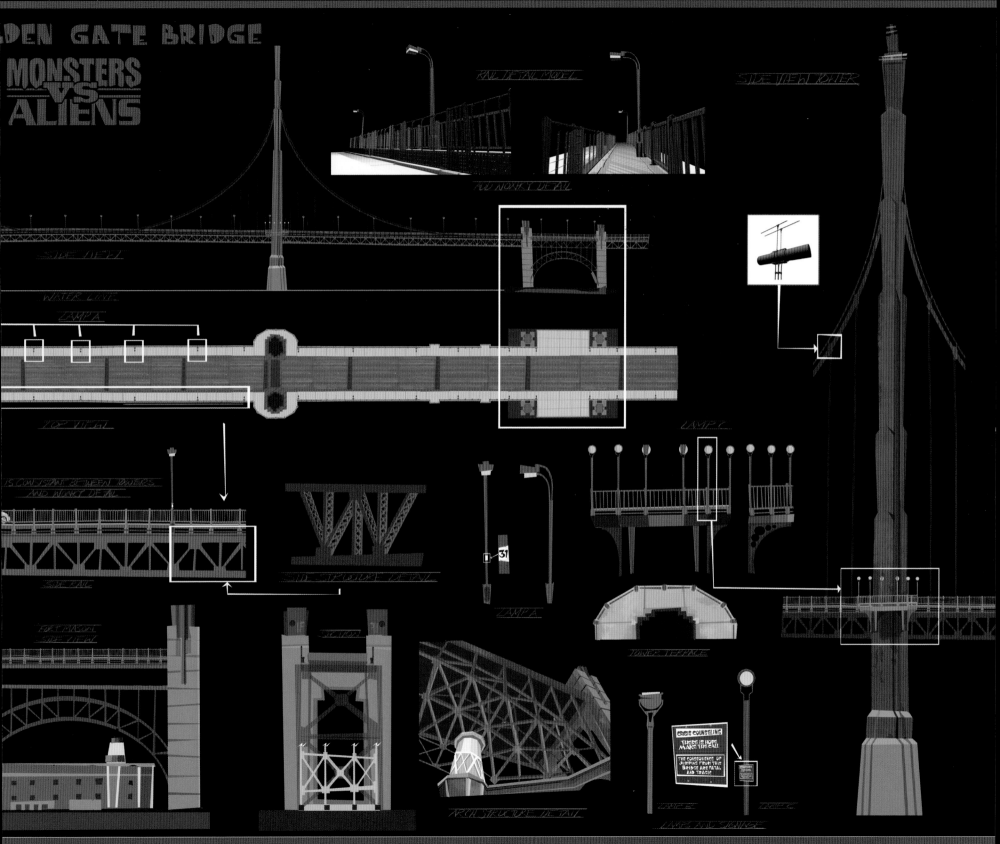

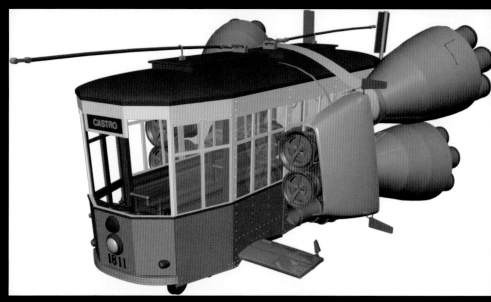

(left) **CG still**. (above) Super Muni—Bret Nystul, Facundo Rabaudi—3D design.

(below) **Flying Truck**—Brett Nystul—3D design.

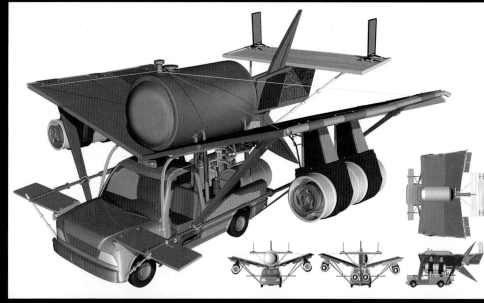

THE MOTHERSHIP: EXTERIOR

The visualization of the Mothership was an enormous challenge because it could take on almost any shape or form. Given such creative license, the designers came up with hundreds of ideas and variations, including the concept of a huge flying gun.

The basic shape of the Mothership was informed by several early digital drawings that helped create an alien space language. According to production designer David James, some of this work was inspired by the contemporary artist Lee Bontecou, whose unique textural style reminded James of a fresh new take on an alien look.

One particular drawing by Patrick Hanenberger was a huge conceptual step forward. The designers describe this painting as looking a bit like an "alien Miami Beach." Hanenberger created it when the villain was an intergalactic oil baron, and it was meant to display Gallaxhar's sense of excess and decadence. Although this concept was abandoned, many of these pale colors and amoeba-like shapes were incorporated into the final look and design of the ship.

Once the basic shape and color were established, different kinds of details such as lights, textures, and antennae were added to give the ship more believability and make it look like it could really fly.

Mothership City Concept—Patrick Hanenberger—digital paint.

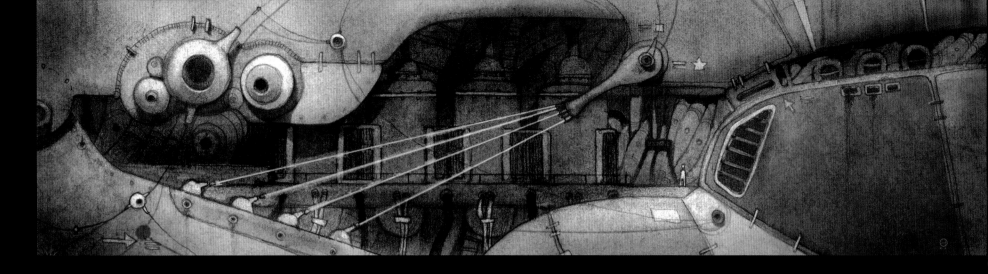

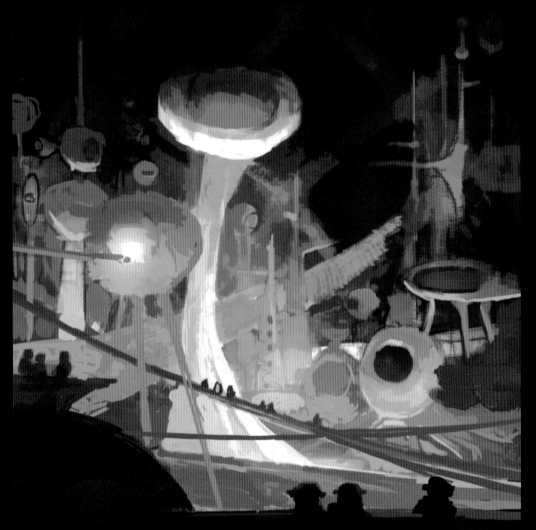

(above) **Mothership Exploration**—Patrick Hanenberger—digital paint

(left) **Mothership City**—Patrick Hanenberger—digital paint.

(below) **Mothership Explorations**—Ritche Sacilioc—digital paint.

(opposite) **Mothership Concepts**—Patrick Hanenberger—digital paint.

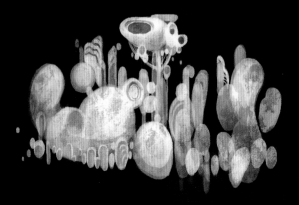

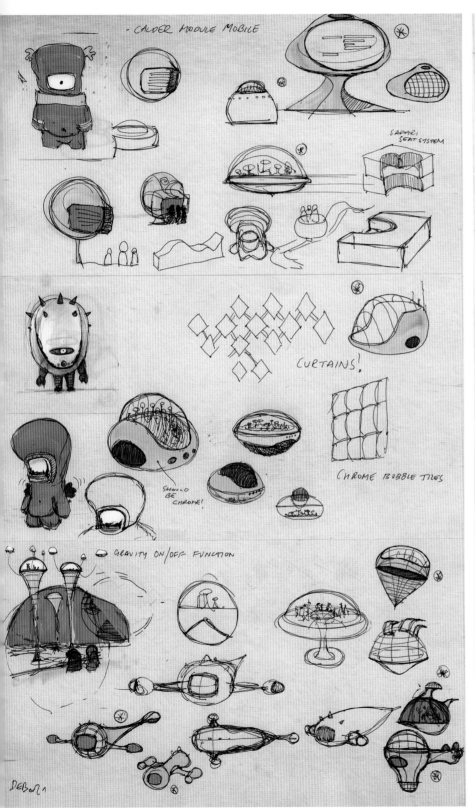

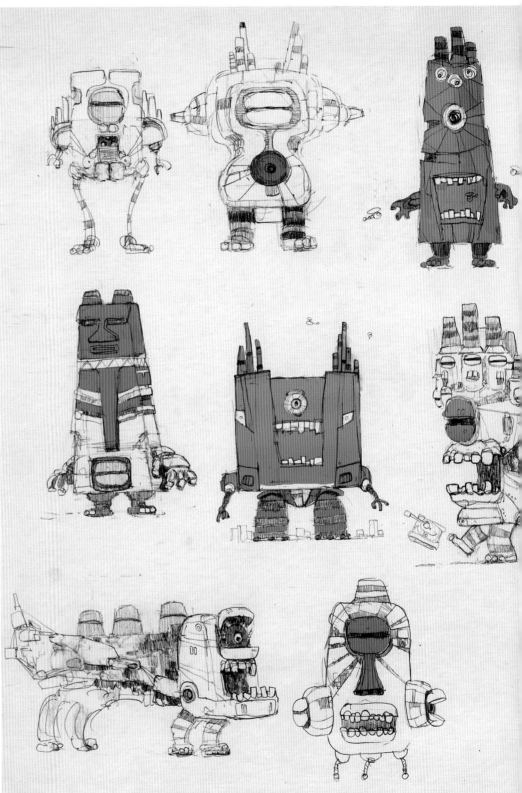

(all) **Alien Aesthetic Ideas**—Patrick Hanenberger—pencil & digital paint.

121

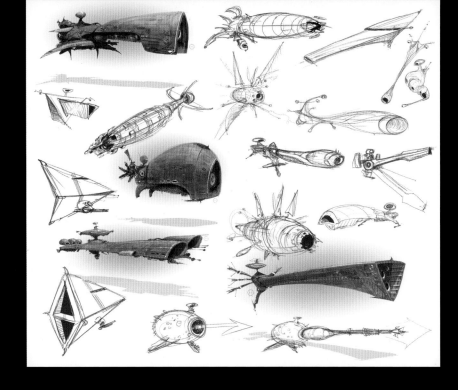

(above) **Mothership Sketches**—Patrick Hanenberger—digital paint. (below) **Mothership 2**—Patrick Hanenberger—digital paint. (right) **Mothership**—Patrick Hanenberger—digital paint.

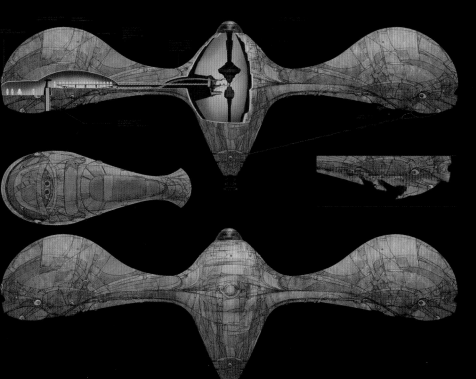

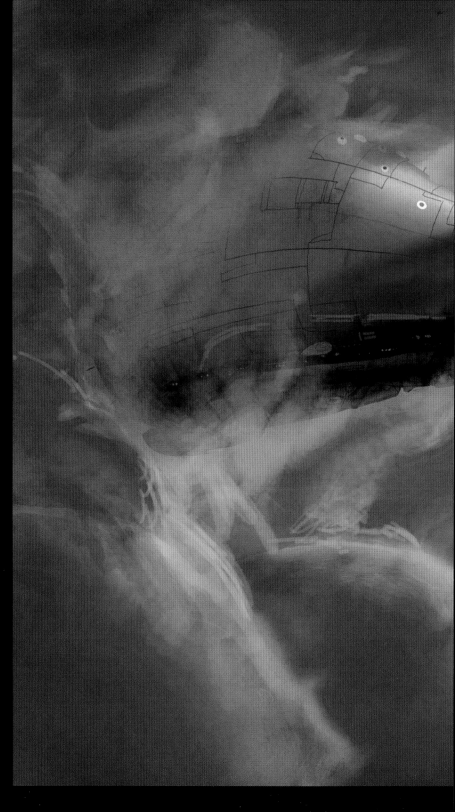

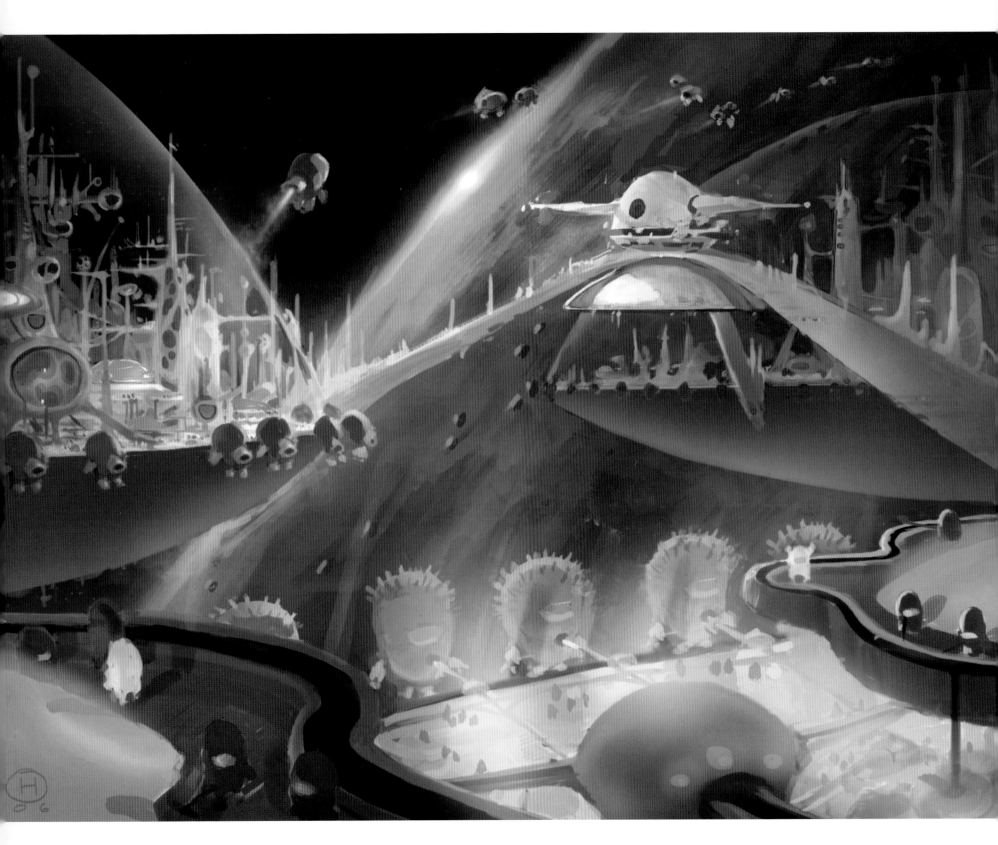

THE MOTHERSHIP: INTERIOR

The interior of the Mothership represented an entirely different challenge from the exterior. Once again, the artists grappled with the problems of scale, size, and proportion. Some of the characters are enormous, and the world inside the ship has to be designed to contain them while still showing their size and scale. Designing a room that could hold the giant robots and a 49-foot-11-inch woman was as difficult in the Mothership as it had been in the Monster Prison.

Originally the interior of the Mothership had an organic feel and a pinkish color. This worked when the villain was a female catlike creature, but certainly was not right for the dark and brooding Gallaxhar. Still, these drawings were useful because the production of a movie like *Monsters vs. Aliens* is an evolutionary process, and these early drawings helped define what did not work. Knowing what's wrong with a design is almost as important as knowing what's right. The decision was made that the interior of the ship needed to be moody and dramatic. Gallaxhar's sleep pod, for example, became a deep, dark purple.

The Mothership included hundreds of working elements, each designed to look both authentic and productive. For example, a great deal of work went into the hangar for the oil-gathering robots, even though this area did not represent a major scene in the film.

Mothership Interior Exploration—Patrick Hanenberger—digital paint.

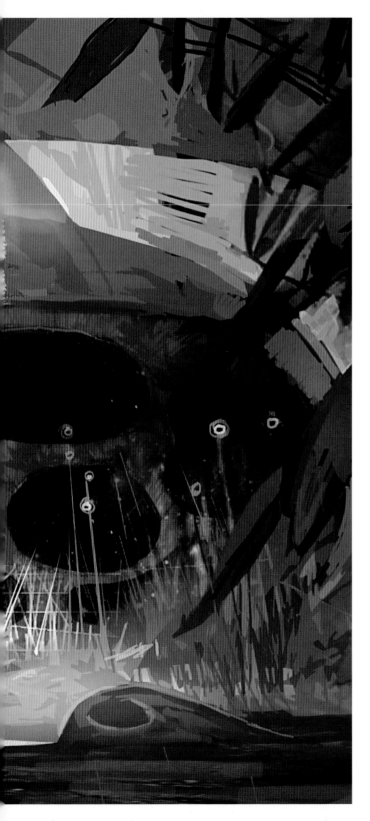

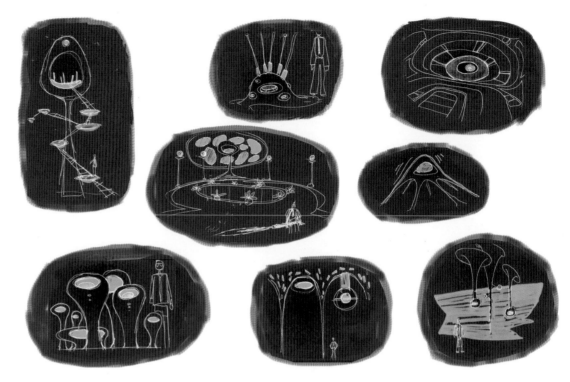

(above) **Mothership Exploration**—Patrick Hanenberger—
pen & digital paint. *(left, right, and below)* **Gallaxhar's Bridge**—
Patrick Hanenberger—digital paint. *(following pages)* **Robot
Hangar Concept**—Patrick Hanenberger—digital paint.

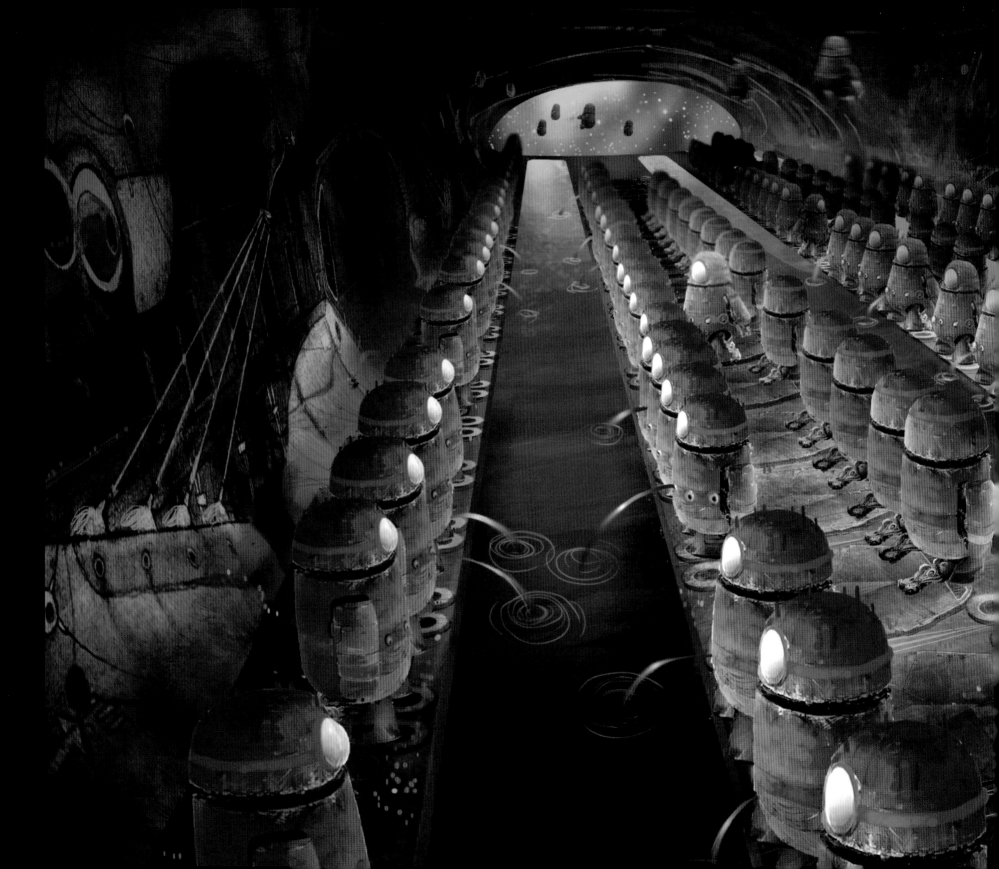

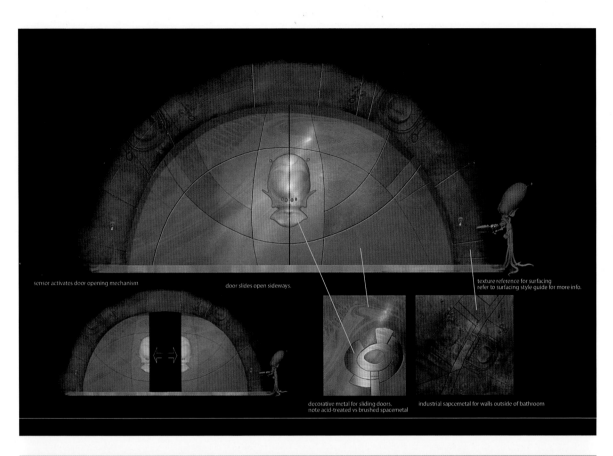

sensor activates door opening mechanism   door slides open sideways.   texture reference for surfacing
                                                                                                refer to surfacing style guide for more info.

decorative metal for sliding doors.   industrial sapcemetal for walls outside of bathroom
note acid-treated vs brushed spacemetal

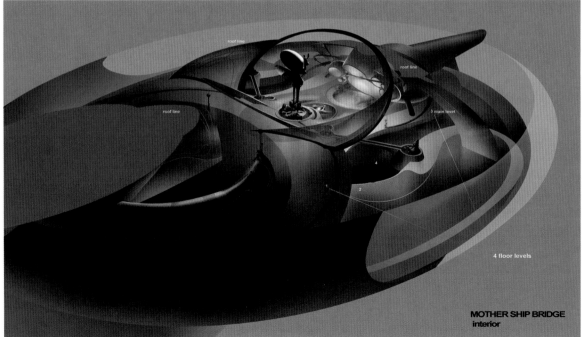

MOTHER SHIP BRIDGE
interior

4 floor levels

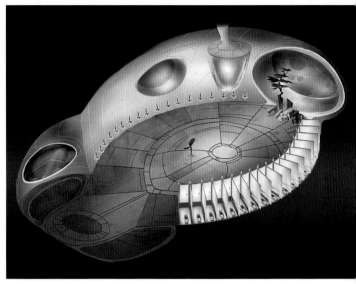

(above left) **Gallaxhar's Bathroom Door**—Patrick Hanenberger—
digital paint. (above) **Gallaxhar's Bathroom**—Patrick Hanenberger—
digital paint. (below left) **Mothership Bridge Interior**—Ritche
Sacilioc—3D design & digital paint. (below) **Gallaxhar's Bridge**—
Ritche Sacilioc—3D design & digital paint.
(opposite above left) **Gallaxhar's Bridge**—Ritche Sacilioc—3D
design & digital paint. (opposite above right) **Gallaxhar's Scooter**—
Brett Nystul—3D design. (opposite below) **Gallaxhar's Sleep Pod**—
Brett Nystul—digital paint & 3D design.

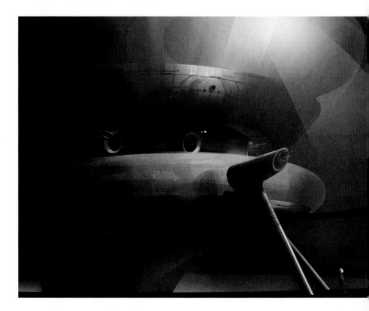

The overall concept for the interior of the mothership was to create a mix between an aircraft carrier, a giant factory, and a floating city.

—PATRICK HANENBERGER, VISUAL DEVELOPMENT ARTIST

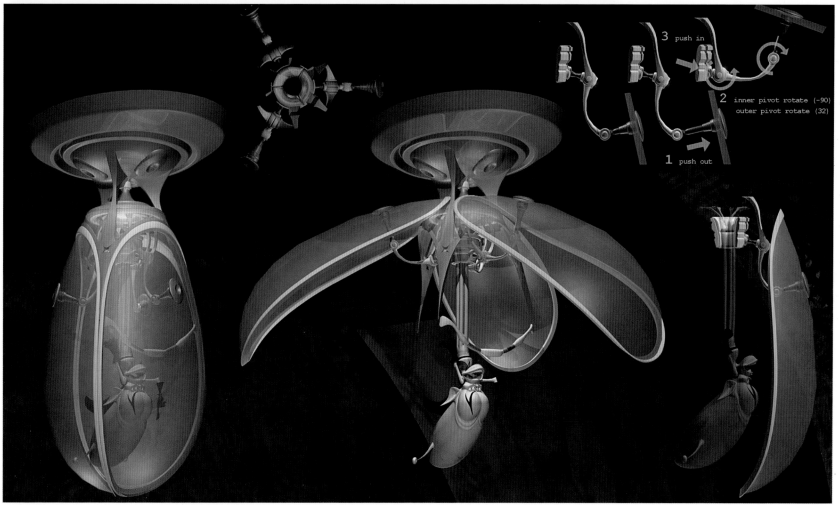

3 push in

2 inner pivot rotate (-90)
outer pivot rotate (32)

1 push out

CAPTURE, EXTRACTION, AND CLONING DEVICES

The Mothership needed essential equipment to perform its tasks on the planet Earth, and these included a capture device to bring Susan onto the ship; an extraction machine to remove the quontonium from her body, a scanner/copier to make duplicates of Gallaxhar, and a cloning device to give life to those duplicates.

Transporting a 49-foot-11-inch Susan up to the Mothership required a special, quite large device that would create an electronic prison to encircle Susan and radiate the energy needed to bring her onboard the ship. The designers gave careful thought to creating a device that looked like it could really work in this situation. For all of these machines, complicated schematic plans were drawn.

The concept of cloning and how to make it look real was an important design element in the creation of the interior of the Mothership.

One of Gallaxhar's most evil plans is to populate the Earth with replicas of himself. To this end, the design team needed to create a sophisticated mechanical system that would show Gallaxhar's cloning process at work and be believable as a workable machine. Many engineering plans were drawn to simulate the kind of equipment that might resemble a working cloning device.

The team created three machines to simulate the cloning process. First was the extraction machine which artist Peter Maynez describes as "a kind of giant juicer." Susan is trapped inside

this machine and all of the quontonium life energy that made her into Ginormica is sucked out of her. Miscellaneous machines above the extraction device transport and store the quontonium while Gallaxhar uses a kind of scanner/copier machine to make copies of himself. These copies are lifeless without the quontonium so it is the function of the cloning machine to breath life into the scanned copies. The cloning machine was designed to look like a giant conveyor belt with pods that stamp out clones of Gallaxhar. These clones were then housed in one of the three major hangars on the Mothership. In the end, the designers accomplished exactly what they set out to do. In a bizarre way, it does feel as though this process could actually work.

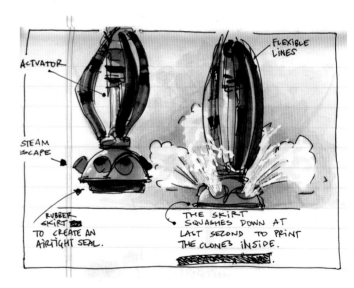

ACTVATOR

FLEXIBLE LINES

STEAM SCAPE

RUBBER SKIRT TO CREATE AN AIRTIGHT SEAL.

THE SKIRT SQUASHES DOWN AT LAST SECOND TO PRINT THE CLONES INSIDE.

(above) **Gallaxhar's Capture Pod**—Brett Nystul—3D design & digital paint. *(above right and opposite top)* **The Cloner**—Peter Maynez—pen & marker. *(opposite below left)* **The Extractor**—Peter Maynez—pen & marker.
(opposite below right) **Mothership Core**—Peter Maynez, Brett Nytsul, Ritche Sacilioc—3D design—Patrick Hanenberger—digital paint.

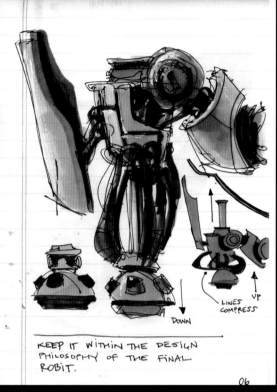

KEEP IT WITHIN THE DESIGN
PHILOSOPHY OF THE FINAL
ROBIT.

DOWN

UP

LINES
COMPRESS

06

PIVOT   PIVOT

PIVOT

PIVOT

• NOT TO SCALE
• FUNCTION/DESIGN ONLY

07

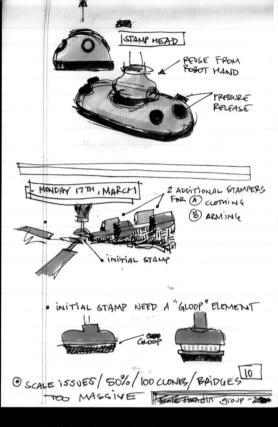

STAMP HEAD

REUSE FROM
ROBOT HAND

PRESSURE
RELEASE

MONDAY 17TH, MARCH

2 ADDITIONAL STAMPERS
FOR Ⓐ CLOTHING
Ⓑ ARMING

INITIAL STAMP

• INITIAL STAMP NEED A "GLOOP" ELEMENT

GLOOP

◉ SCALE ISSUES / 50% / 100 CLONES / BRIDGES
TOO MASSIVE

10

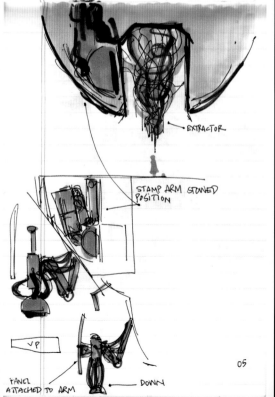

EXTRACTOR

STAMP ARM STOWED
POSITION

VP

PANEL
ATTACHED TO ARM

DOWN

05

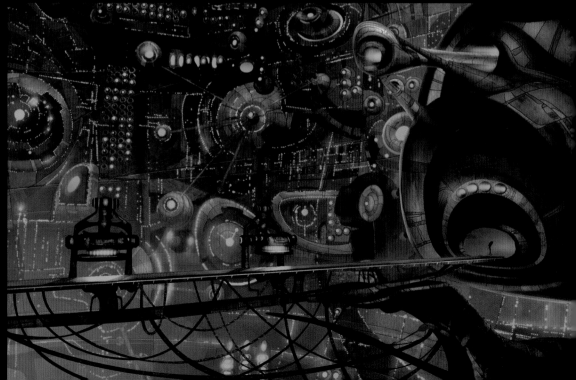

(above) **Mothership Core**—Ritche Sacilioc—digital paint. (left) **Mothership Computer Brain**—Ritche Sacilioc—digital paint & 3D design. (opposite) **Mothership Brainroom**—Ritche Sacilioc—digital paint. (following pages) **The Hangar**—Timothy Lamb—digital paint.

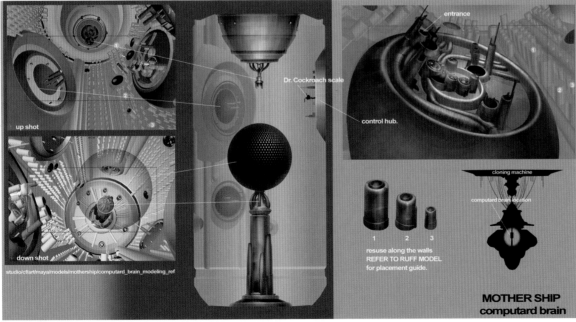

entrance

Dr. Cockroach scale

control hub.

up shot

down shot

studio/cf/art/maya/models/mothership/computard_brain_modeling_ref

cloning machine

computard brain location

1 2 3

resuse along the walls
REFER TO RUFF MODEL
for placement guide.

MOTHER SHIP
computard brain

We wanted the machines in Gallaxhar's mothership to look futuristic, industrial, and clean. They can't be dirty because this is the first time they're being used. Once Gallaxhar captures Susan, he can break the seal on these machines.

—JED SCHLANGER, ART AND MODELING SUPERVISOR

(above) **1800 Key**—Timothy Lamb—digital paint. (below) **1910 Key**—Timothy Lamb—digital paint.

(above) **1925 Key**—Chris Brock—digital paint. (below) **Key**—Richard Daskas—digital paint.

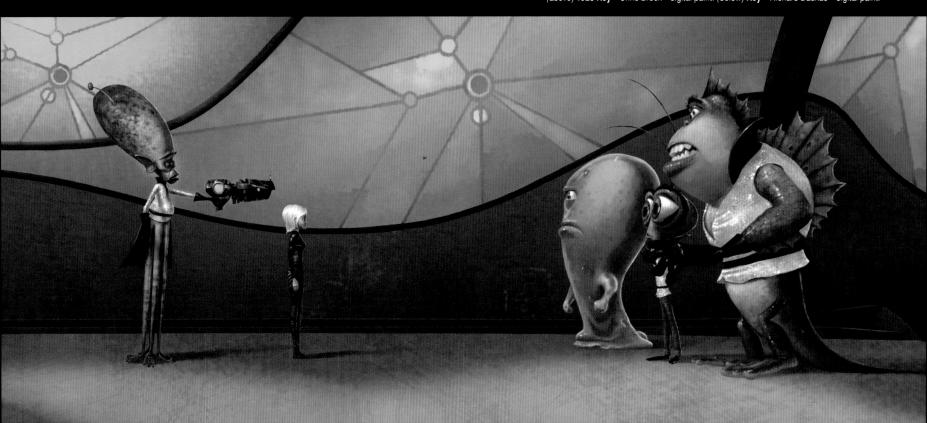

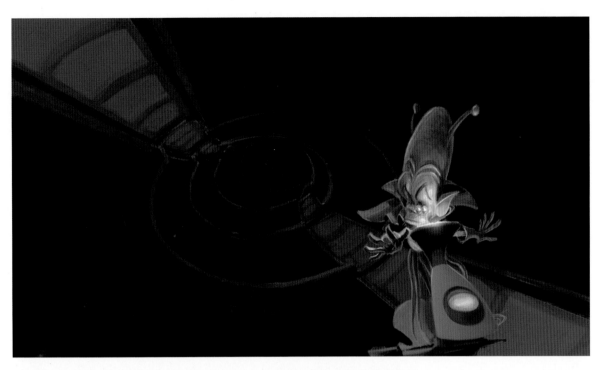

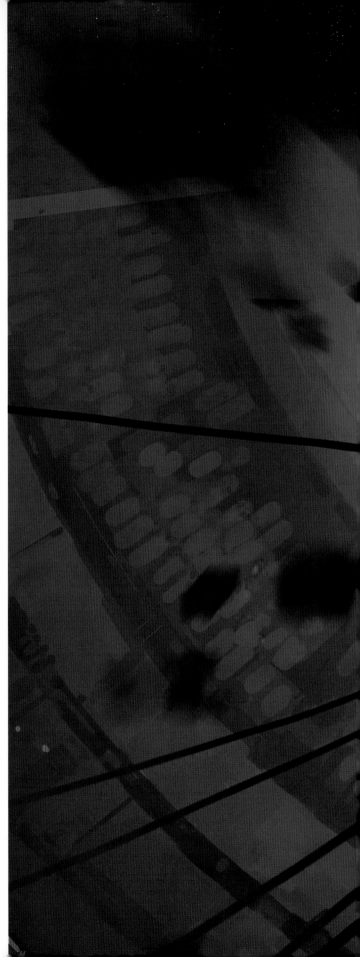

(above and below) **Tunnel Keys**—Ronald Kurniawan—digital paint. (right) **Key**—Ritche Sacilioc—digital paint.

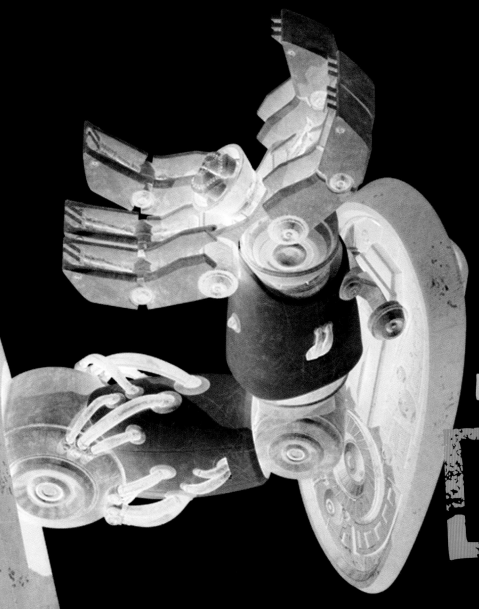

PART THREE
SPECIAL F/X

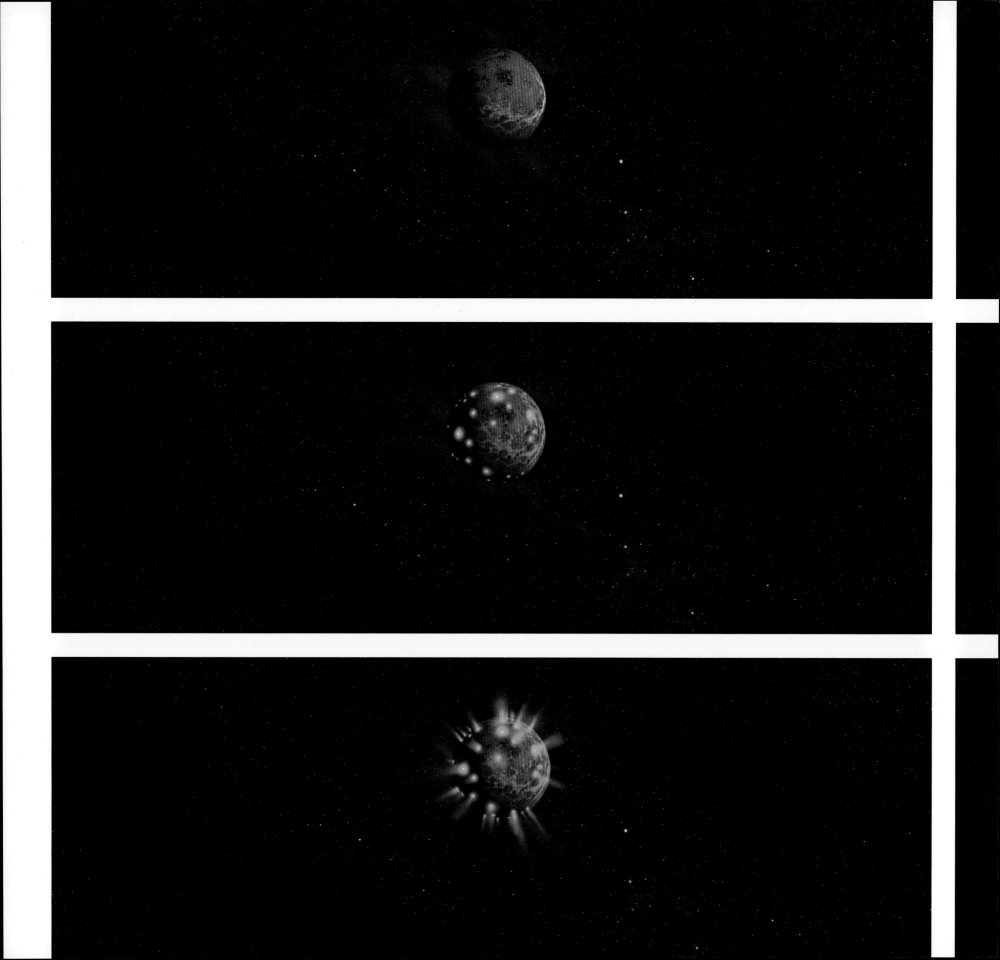

EXPLODING PLANET

The art department creates the look of the characters, the environments, and the props; the story department writes and develops the story. It is the job of the effects department to take these visions and ideas and make them come to life on the screen.

"The paintings and drawings from the art department are our starting-off points," says Yancy Lindquist, head of effects. "We work on everything that moves but is not a character. This includes all the props, explosions, buildings breaking apart, storms, dust clouds, even the plant life. We take the art and make it work in a 3-D space. Sometimes the final effect is very close to the original art, sometimes it morphs into something very different."

Monsters vs. Aliens opens with a big effects scene. Even before the story officially starts, as a kind of prologue, we witness the explosion of an entire planet in deep space. We see the planet rupture, explode, and break apart; a meteor breaks off and travels toward Earth.

The destruction of the planet was planned in three basic stages. First, the planet would begin to crack and fracture. Next, we would see the

Exploding Planet—Richard Daskas—digital paint.

145

actual explosion where the fissures radiate and the planet breaks apart. Finally, there are shock waves and flying pieces of debris from inside the planet, creating a ring around the planet that seems to radiate towards the audience. Shafts of light, molten debris and flying sparks are part of the final effect.

For the F/X department, the effects in this scene (and in all subsequent scenes) were made even more spectacular because of the 3-D technology that was part of the filmmaking from the very start. The technology enhanced every explosion and made the visuals more dynamic. All the scenes involving fire were far more realistic in feel and emotion. Particles that rained down from the sky had density and weight. Dust fields were real enough to reach out and touch. The technology helped put the audience next to the exploding planet in a unique and remarkable way.

FIRST CONTACT F/X

The original paintings for the scene where humans first encounter the aliens can't begin to show the impact that will be created by the effects. But the process begins with the art department passing along an image for the effects department to follow.

"First Contact" was the first big 3-D stereoscopic sequence created by the filmmakers, and for the effects department it was a chance to explore how to use the technology in an action sequence. "We took what was given to us from the art department and had to figure out how to incorporate the stereoscopic element," explains Yancy Lindquist, head of effects. "We worked on missile trails, fire from the missiles, and explosions coming out of the robot. The artwork had a lot of saturated color and detail that made the explosion look massive, and we worked hard to maintain those details."

Another example of how the art department informs the effects department is in the creation of the substance known as quontonium. This glowing green meteor was created by the art department to indicate how the material should radiate. It was up to special effects to add the glow effect.

> In "First Contact" we positioned the missile trails to get a stereo "WOW" effect for the shot.
> —YANCY LINDQUIST, HEAD OF EFFECTS

(above) **Exploding Planet**—Richard Daskas—digital paint. *(above right)* **Meteor**—Patrick Hanenberger—digital paint. *(opposite above)* **Stills**. *(opposite below)* **First Contact Explosion**—Scott Wills—digital paint.

THE FORCE FIELD AND THE ROBOT BEAM

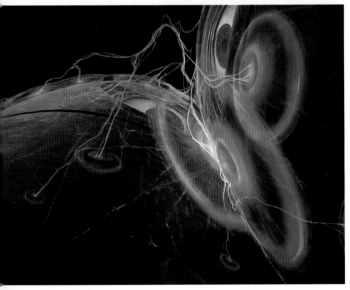

During the "First Contact" sequence, the military fires on the robot only to discover he is protected by a force field. The art department supplied artwork for the look of the protective field. "That is one instance where we matched the artwork that was supplied," says Lindquist. "The art showed the explosion with a nice sculpting of the fire that we mimicked. We also played up the great trails of fire in 3-D with the fire coming toward the camera."

As for the robot beam, this effect was meant to enhance the light that emanates from the cy-

clops eye of the alien robot. "We took the art and gave it a feel to show that the light from the eye beam was gathering information," says Lindquist. "We added a lot of details like rings, sonar pulses, and swirly patterns. This is one instance where it came back with a request to simplify the effect. So we pulled back and took off some of the details. We wound up with a few pulsating, extruded rings and a glistening kind of light. In the end, though, the effect came out much like the original piece of art we started with."

(top) **Robot Force Field**—Scott Wills—digital paint. *(above)* **Force Fields Colliding**—Ronald Kurniawan—digital paint. *(opposite above left)* **Shield Lighting Effect**—CG still. *(opposite above right)* **Final Shield Image**—CG still. *(opposite below)* **Robot Beam**—Richard Daskas—digital paint.

148

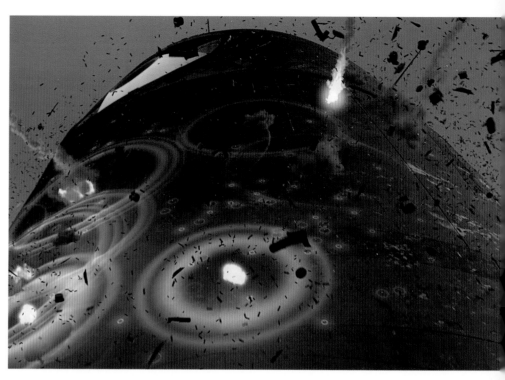

TAKING DOWN THE GOLDEN GATE BRIDGE

San Francisco is the location for the first big action scene in the movie, and it involves a great many effects, including the destruction of the Golden Gate Bridge. But, like any other sequence, the action has to serve the story.

"Any action scene is going to be boring if you're not invested in the characters," explains head of story Peter Ramsey. "Action scenes are not just about action—they are story scenes with action in them, and they need the same structure as any dramatic scene. We always start with knowing who our characters are and defining what they want, so that every scene reflects a particular aspect of that. It took us many different iterations to understand that the action scene in San Francisco is really about Susan realizing that, as a result of her new identity, she has a lot more inner strength than she thought. Specifically, she discovers the untapped depth

she could not access before she grew into Ginormica, and it turns the key in her psyche."

At the start of the scene, Susan runs away from the confrontation because she doesn't think she can fight back. "She is forced into action when the robot claw clamps down on her," continues Ramsey. "At first it looks like she's crushed, but then she almost reflexively pushes the claw open and realizes she is much stronger than she thought. She can survive this fight. Maybe she can even use her newfound strength to her advantage. This is a defining moment for the character."

The destruction of the Golden Gate Bridge was always conceived so that it would break as realistically as possible. The look of the destruction was carefully planned long before it went into effects. "We worked closely with layout and with [layout supervisor] Damon O'Beirne to pre-

(left) **Insecto In San Fran**—Richard Daskas—digital paint. *(above)* **San Fran Key**—Timothy Lamb—digital paint.

visualize the destruction," explains visual effects supervisor Ken Bielenberg. "Layout took a rough first pass, and effects took it further to show what could be done with snapping cables and crumbling asphalt. They worked on how the bridge would snap when the robot went through it. Then we passed it back to the camera people. The destruction of the bridge is our hero shot, our money sequence."

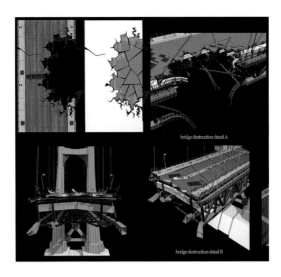

bridge destruction detail A

bridge destruction detail B

The art for the scene went to effects from the art department with a schematic diagram showing how the bridge would break apart in real life. "Though it wasn't specific to the camera angle, it gave us an idea of the complexity involved," says Yancy Lindquist.

Many exciting special effects were added to the scene where the bridge actually starts to deform and then breaks apart. The f/x department created a system for the cables to start to vibrate and then snap apart in a scary, realistic manner. Then the various chunks and pieces of asphalt fall into the water. "We had to create a shallow water fluid simulation to get a realistic

splash motion," explains Lindquist. "After the destruction, we created many different layers of dust and debris to fill out the volume and to make the whole area look dirty."

As the bridge breaks apart, the cars begin to slide, skid, and slam into the railings. Smoke trails from the tail pipes; sparks off the tires were added to increase the level of realism. "The effect for this sequence is to emphasize both the danger of the situation and the scale of the monsters," says Lindquist. "If we do our job, the audience will believe in the imminent danger and realize that these creatures really are huge. We try to get their hearts pumping."

(above) **Bridge Destruction**—Rachel Tiep-Daniels—3D design & digital paint. *(below, right)* **Bridge Damage**—Rachel Tiep-Daniels—3D design.

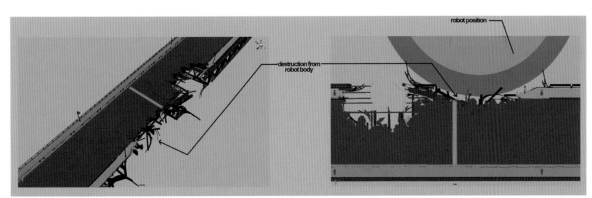

robot position

destruction from robot body

(above) **Bridge Battle**—Chris Brock—digital paint. *(below)* **Ambient Occlution Sims**— David Allen *(following pages)* **CG still**.

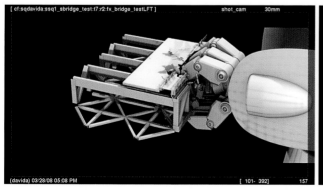

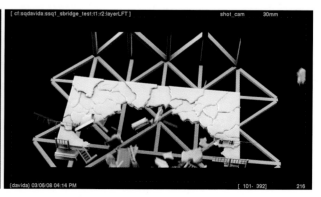

153

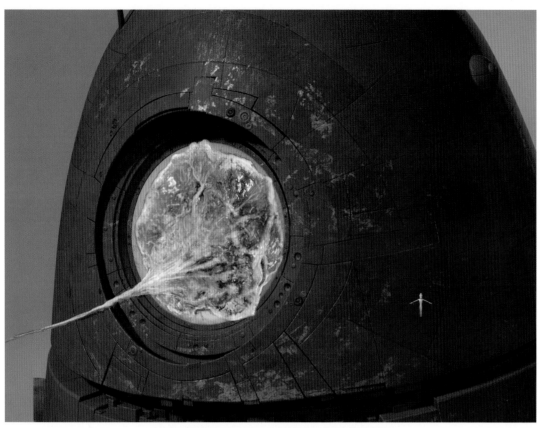

INSECTOSAURUS SNOT

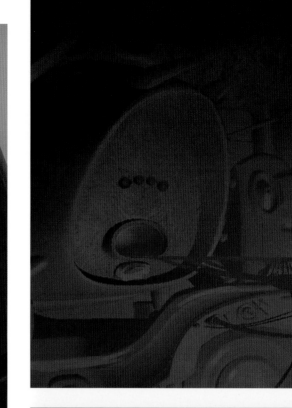

Insectosaurus Snot is one of the most definitive gross-out, geek jokes in *Monsters vs. Aliens*. The "saved by snot" joke takes place when Insectosaurus faces off with the enormous robot alien, on opposite sides of the Golden Gate Bridge.

Insectosaurus is clearly not as strong or mean as the alien robot, but she does have one superpower the alien lacks: She can project snot from her nose, and she does this to great effect, right into the alien's one eye, blinding him long enough so that Susan can crawl away. It is a seminal moment when Insectosaurus discovers her own strength and super talents.

"The artwork sent down to us from the art department changed quite a bit because of the way we had to animate it," explains Yancy. "We used the image for its great color and texture. But after talking to Ken Bielenberg and David James, we decided to animate it by imitating Silly String in terms of how the snot would move and land on the robot. The end look was much more motion-driven to get the coolest effect we could. Here the artwork served mainly as our inspiration."

(above) **Insecto Snot Design**—Ronald Kurniawan—digital paint.

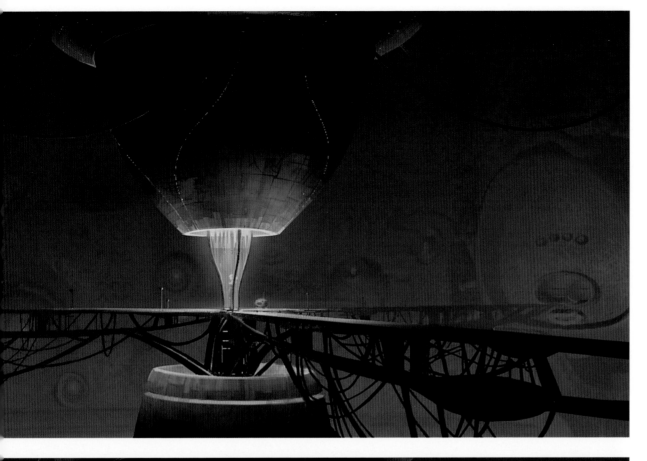

THE EXTRACTION CHAMBER

Following the destruction of the Golden Gate Bridge, Susan returns to her hometown of Modesto in the hopes of reuniting with Derek. She is devastated when he rejects her, and she winds up sitting on a gas station. Her mood is just beginning to shift from heartbroken girl-friend to empowered monster right before Gal-laxhar's Mothership swoops down and pulls her up into the ship.

Gallaxhar needs to extract the quontonium from Susan in order to use it to breathe life into his clones, and the art department had to devise a machine that would serve that purpose. "The Extraction Chamber is shaped like a wine-glass that fans open and traps her inside," says Lindquist. She is imprisoned by bands of light that glow a deep neon shade of green.

Once inside the chamber, the quontonium is extracted from Susan in a process that artist Peter Maynez likens to juicing an orange. In other words, squeezing Susan until the quonto-nium starts to flow. While the art department created a machine that looked like bands of light squeezing the material out of Susan, the effects department gave life and rhythm to that light. They added movement and sparks to make the process look all the more realistic.

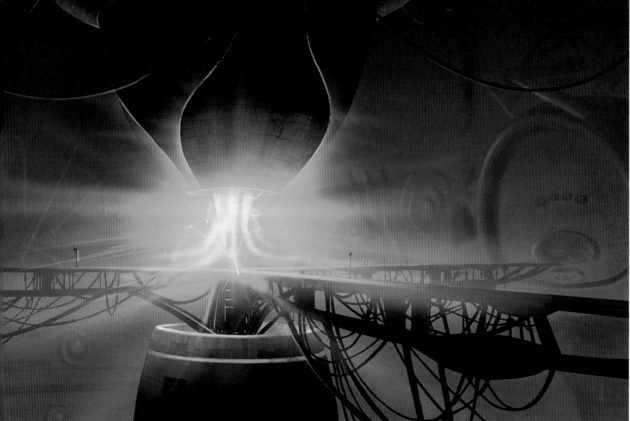

(left above) **Extraction 1**—Timothy Lamb—digital paint—Brett Nystul, Peter Maynez—3D design. (left below) **Extraction 2**—Timothy Lamb—digital paint—Brett Nystul, Peter Maynez—3D design.

157

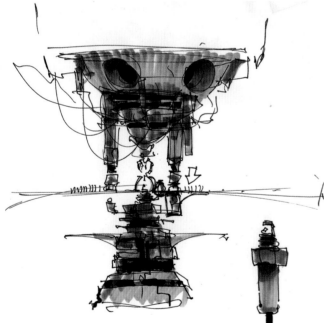

(above) **Core Sketch**—Peter Maynez—pen & marker. **Traveling**

Quontonium Sequence—Ritche Sacilioc—digital paint.

MOTHERSHIP DESTRUCTION

The final climactic battle, which ends with the destruction of the Mothership, is also the defining sequence when Susan and the monsters hit their stride. "They've been locked up for fifty years," says Peter Ramsey. "They are out of shape, kind of rusty, and have been lamenting their old glory days throughout the film. In the final battle, we get to see them collectively take down the Mothership."

For the effects department, the destruction of the Mothership was a golden opportunity to take everything they'd learned working in 3-D to give the movie a powerful conclusion. "This is our last big effect, and we want to make sure it cements the effects in everyone's mind," says Lindquist. "For this sequence, we worked with some cool ideas about how the Mothership might break and explode. We were trying to improve upon our existing techniques to get more realistic detail and more fluid motion in our explosions." The 3-D technology allowed for more believable trails of smoke, particle explosions and more electrical effects. Simply put, it greatly enhanced what was already there on the screen but might not be seen by the audience.

Working in stereoscopic changed the way

the effects department went about their job. "Two things changed," says Yancy Lindquist. "First, we looked for opportunities to take advantage of volume and dimension in the effects. Secondly, we worked hard to avoid what we called 'stereo artifacts.' These include the fact that if we moved too fast on screen, the image would flicker. If we got too close-up, it created eye strain. So, working in 3-D meant concentrating on what we could get and what we needed to avoid."

The great advantage is that 3-D technology puts the viewer inside the movie and is much more than just a gimmick whereby objects are thrown at the audience. "The 3-D experience is supposed to make every character more real and more personal," explains Phil McNally, stereoscopic supervisor. "The audience is literally engaged and looking into the world of the characters on the screen. And that world is coming out to meet the audience as well, so we are closing the gap between the audience and the characters on the screen. These are no longer distant images; they are real and tangible. We can use the 3-D technology to enhance any kind of emotion from peril to sorrow." From the sheer density of the falling snowflakes at the opening of the movie to the aggressive explosions of the final climatic battle, the audience is completely immersed in both the action and the emotion of every scene.

(above) **Finale Concept**—Timothy Lamb—digital paint. *(opposite and following pages)* **Mothership Explosion**—Ritche Sacilioc—digital paint.

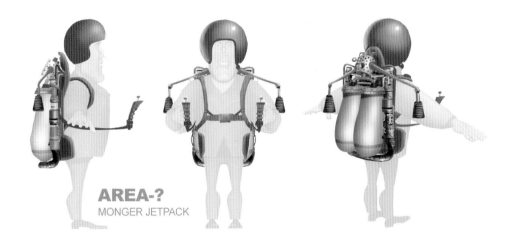

AREA-?
MONGER JETPACK

PROPS: MILITARY VEHICLES, TANKS, AND GUNS

"Our task, as visual development artists, is to give the objects in the film a reason to be there and a believability," says visual development artist Patrick Hanenberger. "The objects we design are not just in the film to be funny or scary. We give them a back story and add dimension to their existence. We create visuals that are not only cool, but that add to the story line and make it more enjoyable."

Many different vehicles and armaments—both terrestrial and extraterrestrial—were required for this film. Each truck, car, bus, and handgun had to be conceived and created. The concept for these pieces had to fit with the general design initiative of the movie—that is, they needed to be realistic but with a stylized edge.

To accomplish this, Patrick Hanenberger took model kits and made the military tanks and planes; then he changed their scale and proportion. For example, on the planes, he ex-

panded the size of the cockpit and the wings while keeping the basic size of the scale model. This made the vehicle or plane look like it had a huge head and disproportionate limbs, which was the basic design for the human characters in the film. In this way, he made the objects fit the skewed proportions of the characters. "The tank is twice as tall and chubby, and we added clutter everywhere," says Hanenberger. Hanenberger applied the same basic techniques to create the tanks and cars.

Other weapons for the military were made in a super-exaggerated style so that they would not feel threatening. Their size and goofy shape tilt them away from being scary and toward being humorous.

The effects department enhanced all the vehicles and weapons by adding dust when the tanks rolled through the desert, or smoke and muzzle fire when the guns were fired.

(above) **Monger's Jetpack**—Patrick Hanenberger—digital paint. *(right)* **Crash Site Jets**—Patrick Hanenberger—digital paint.

(top) **Transport Plane**—Facundo Raubadi—3D design & digital paint. (above) **Apache Helicopter**—Patrick Hanenberger—digital paint.

(below left) **Tank**—Patrick Hanenberger—digital paint. (below right) **Military Vehicle**—Ritche Sacilioc—digital paint.

We looked at existing tanks, aircraft, and military vehicles and then made them into caricatures in the same way that the humans in the film were exaggerated into caricatures.

—PATRICK HANENBERGER, VISUAL DEVELOPMENT ARTIST

(above) **Guns**—Ronald Kurniawan—digital paint.

(left) **Various Weapons**—Michael Isaak—digital paint.

(right) **Rocket Launcher**—Rachel Tiep-Daniels—digital paint & 3d-Design. *(below)* **Guns 2**—Ronald Kurniawan—digital paint.

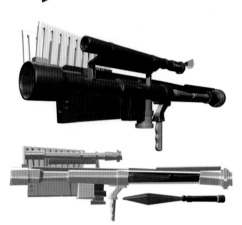

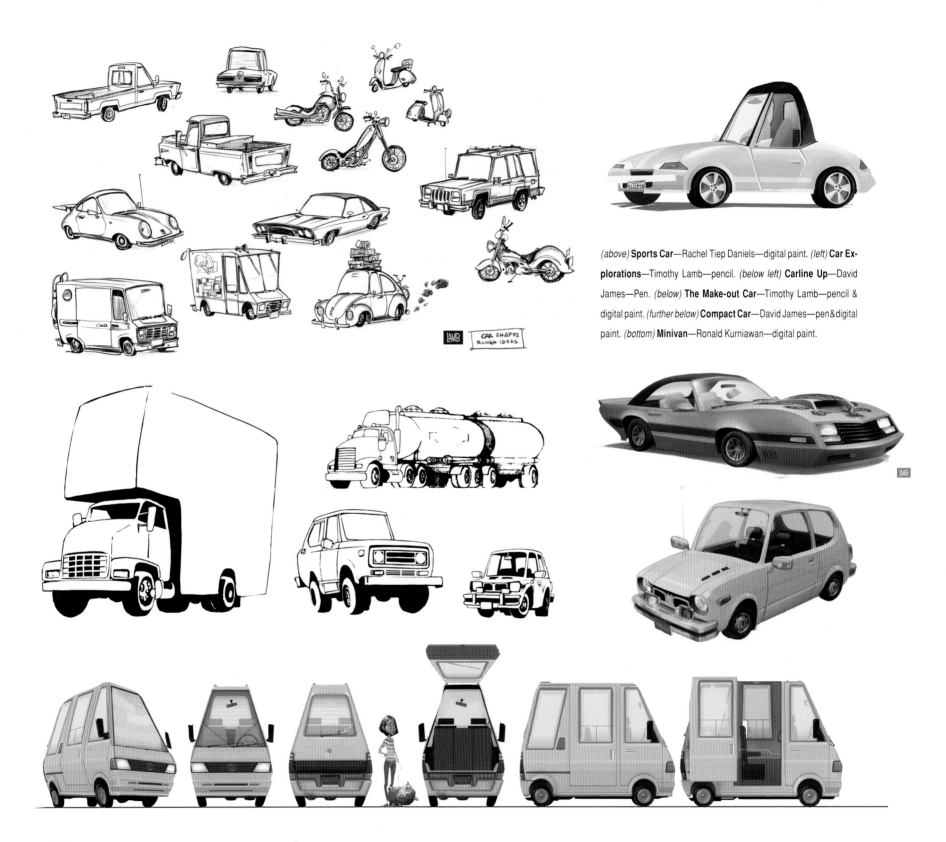

(above) **Sports Car**—Rachel Tiep Daniels—digital paint. (left) **Car Explorations**—Timothy Lamb—pencil. (below left) **Carline Up**—David James—Pen. (below) **The Make-out Car**—Timothy Lamb—pencil & digital paint. (further below) **Compact Car**—David James—pen&digital paint. (bottom) **Minivan**—Ronald Kurniawan—digital paint.

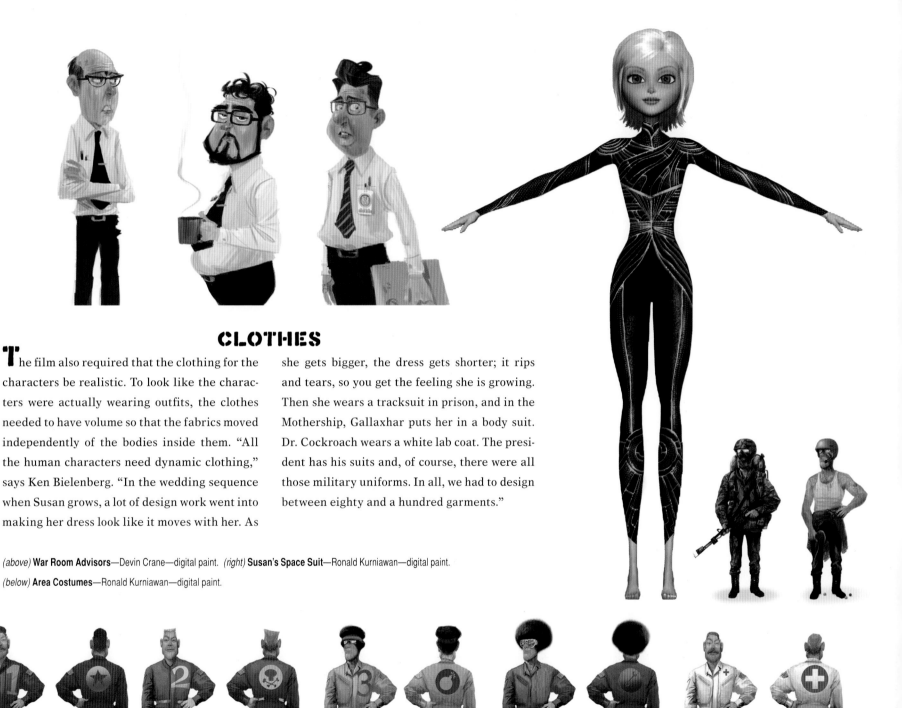

CLOTHES

The film also required that the clothing for the characters be realistic. To look like the characters were actually wearing outfits, the clothes needed to have volume so that the fabrics moved independently of the bodies inside them. "All the human characters need dynamic clothing," says Ken Bielenberg. "In the wedding sequence when Susan grows, a lot of design work went into making her dress look like it moves with her. As she gets bigger, the dress gets shorter; it rips and tears, so you get the feeling she is growing. Then she wears a tracksuit in prison, and in the Mothership, Gallaxhar puts her in a body suit. Dr. Cockroach wears a white lab coat. The president has his suits and, of course, there were all those military uniforms. In all, we had to design between eighty and a hundred garments."

(above) **War Room Advisors**—Devin Crane—digital paint. *(right)* **Susan's Space Suit**—Ronald Kurniawan—digital paint.

(below) **Area Costumes**—Ronald Kurniawan—digital paint.

PART FOUR

THE MAKING OF

DreamWorks
MONSTERS
VS
ALIENS

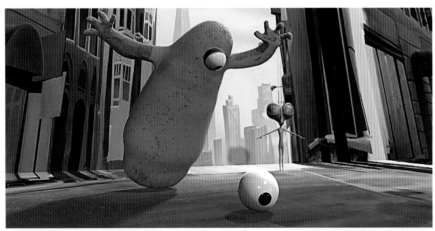

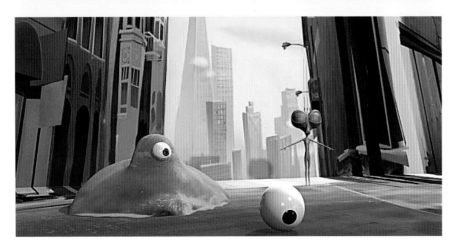

RIGGING AND ANIMATING

For every department, B.O.B. was a singular challenge, especially when it came to rigging. *Rigging* is the process that will give movement to a character and determine which body parts will move, in what direction, and to what angle. Rigging creates a kind of three-dimensional skeleton for a character upon which an exterior skin can be added. The problem with a character like B.O.B. is that he has no rigid lines, so figuring out exactly what he can and can't do takes a great deal of thought and preparation. Whatever decisions get made about his mobility and flexibility, these have to be consistent throughout the entire film.

"B.O.B. doesn't have shoulders, so his arms can pop out of his head or anywhere else in his body," explains David Burgess, head of charac-

ter animation. "He can turn into a puddle, and sometimes he needs to look like he's dripping. His eyeball has to rotate around his head. On the easy side, he is basically a big head—an eyeball and a mouth—so we can get a really fun performance from him."

For all his flexibility, though, the animators needed to have control over the character and claim his boundaries. "B.O.B. was a big development task for the character animators who needed to get character reads," explains Ken Bielenberg. "We had to combine his face system with a system for his goopiness. We also had to come up with the right look for his transparency and complexity within his goopiness."

B.O.B. was in development longer than any other character in the movie. "He was much

(*above and left*) **B.O.B. Development**—Scott Cegielski.

173

more difficult than an opaque character," says Bielenberg.

Another very difficult element on this film (and on most animated features) is the creation of hair. Real hair does not move in a solid mass—it is the aggregate of thousands of strands. Without individual strand movement, hair will look like a hat. This is not so much a problem for creating a cartoon character, but if the directive is that the character be as realistic as possible, then someone has to figure out how to animate hair.

In the beginning, Susan's hair was short and sassy, but as the character designers gave her longer and longer hair, they created more problems for the animators. "Early on, Susan's hair was simple and dynamic but it felt like a helmet, so we had to redesign it and come up with a new animation system to add motion to her hair," says Ken Bielenberg. "Her look is more realistic, so it required natural-looking hair, and because

they wanted longer hair, it had to interact with her shoulders."

At first Susan is a brunette, but after she is hit with alien goop, her hair turns platinum blonde, which created even more problems for the lighting and animating departments. "It's been a huge challenge to make Susan's hair look real," admits Scott Wills. "She's a platinum-white blonde, which already looks fake. Her hair is long and she is doing all this action stuff, so her hair has to move in realistic ways."

Equally complicated was creating the way Susan would move. How does a 49-foot-11-inch-tall woman walk? Big people walk entirely differently from little people.

Susan needed to project her size while walking so that we never lose the sense of her height, but she also needed to look attractive in the process. This was harder to accomplish than one might think. "We tweaked Susan until she became a little more realistic. She had to be

more real in order for the audience to relate to her," explains David Burgess. "As far as animation, even though she is almost fifty feet tall, she can't be lumbering around. Conversely, she can't move like a six-foot person, either. She needed weight and mass. So up close she moves more or less normally, but when the camera pulls back, you get a sense of her size and she takes more time to get around. Susan is our most realistic character in terms of animation."

(above) **Uniform Exploration**—Ronald Kurniawan—digital paint. *(above right)* **Susan Hairstyles**—Devin Crane digital paint. *(below right)* **CG still**. *(facing page top)* **CG still**. *(facing page bottom)* **San Fran Key**—Timothy Lamb—digital paint.

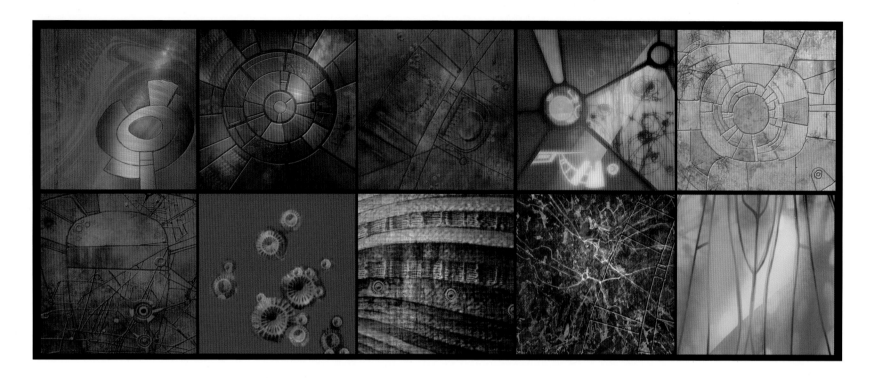

SURFACING AND LIGHTING

Surfacing is the process of adding texture to the characters and environments, and includes everything from creating a beard for the face of the president to inventing an alien version of transparent glass for the windows in the Mothership. Dozens of people contributed to this stage of production.

The face of the president is, in fact, a good example of surfacing, and one that was particularly complex. "The president's face is pushed designwise, but the surfacing is probably more realistic than you've ever seen before," says art director Scott Wills. "From the stubble of his beard to the blood vessels in his nose, every element is totally real-looking. In this kind of movie, you would assume the surfacing would be stylized, but this style ties them to the real world, even though they are really goofy."

Surfacing also applies to all things mechanical and all things alien. For the alien robots and the Mothership, a basic palette of alien materials was created and then used to surface different areas. These included such imagined construction materials as glass, ceramics, and metal. Using the same materials throughout the ship gave the film a consistency that added a realistic aspect to the design. The work is extremely detailed and includes adding realistic scratches, paint chipping, space fungus, mold and alien barnacles to the surface of the ship.

The basic color palette of the movie was created to be as realistic as possible and helped enhance the idea of creating a real world that is slightly askew.

"When you are stylized, you can have any color you want. The colors really don't have to make sense, but they look cool," explains Wills. "But we came back to more realistic colors to make the world more realistic. This helped the humor because our characters are stylized, but the threats are very real in their realistic world."

The color of the sky in the San Francisco chase scene, for example, went through many dif-

> Natural but dramatic
> colors work much better
> with the 3-D world.
> —SCOTT WILLS, ART DIRECTOR

(above) **Mothership Texture Library**—Patrick Hanenberger—digital paint. *(facing page)* **Mothership Core**—Patrick Hanenberger—digital paint—Brett Nystul, Peter Maynez, Ritche Sacilioc—3D design.

ferent shades. Though the color is never really a sky blue, it is always within a natural hue.

To ensure that every department knew what colors were required, color key scripts were created fairly early on in the production so that everyone would use the same basic palette.

Lighting each scene is a separate and complex process that follows surfacing. Every scene has to pass through the lighting department, and it is here where every element of every scene is enhanced in the same way that all live-action movies go through a lighting process. Light and shadows can especially affect the sense of size and scale that was so crucial to this production.

The most difficult color for the artists to achieve—and to light—was the color of human skin, especially since the style of this movie required very real-looking skin. "We set out to combine a caricature shape with realistic texture, but we were not sure how that would work

because we hadn't seen it before," says Ken Bielenberg. "Realistic human skin is difficult and sensitive, because the human eye knows how light reacts to skin and it can get plastic-looking really quickly."

As for lighting the characters, by far the greatest challenge was the gelatinous mass known as B.O.B. "Because B.O.B. is transparent, you can see reflections in him," explains Scott Wills. "But you don't want too many reflections, or else he will disappear. We have to be able to look at him, not his reflections, so he can't be too transparent. We have to determine how he will take the light, especially when he is wet. We have to make sure his expressions won't disappear because of his transparency."

How transparent is too transparent? The lighting department grappled with that question for more than a year.

(left) **San Fran Color Treatment**—Timothy Lamb—digital paint—David James—layout. *(above)* **CG still.** *(facing page top 2 rows)* **Act 1 Colorscript Panels**—Scott Wills & Timothy Lamb—digital paint. *(facing page bottom 3 rows)* **Misc Colorscript Panels**—Scott Wills & Timothy Lamb—digital paint.

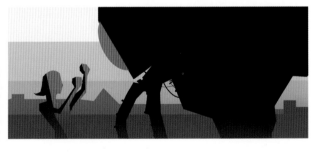  

WORKING IN 3-D

The history of 3-D films dates back to a boom in the mid-1950s when they had a short but popular life in movie theaters. From 1952 to 1953, more than fifty 3-D movies were made in a period of only eighteen months, and then production died off. So many movies made so quickly meant that most of them were shot without much thought, preparation, or artistry. Many of the films from that era were low-budget, relying mostly on the gimmick of 3-D.

Toward the end of the 1970s and into the early 1980s, a handful of 3-D movies were made, and then nothing was produced (aside from educational documentaries) until a few recent arrivals.

In recent history, the 3-D movies that were made for 3-D projection were shot in 2-D and then turned over to the 3-D department. This is akin to shooting in black and white and then handing the movie over to the color department, where color is slapped on but was never part of the thinking, design, or emotional pacing of the film.

"For *Monsters vs. Aliens*, Jeffrey Katzenberg asked us to author in 3-D. That meant we were looking for shots for the purposes of storytelling and the spatial opportunities of this new media," says stereoscopic supervisor Phil McNally. "We took the notion of a spatial media all the way back to the beginning of production. Since almost the very beginning, we have been actively discussing what is 2-D and what is 3-D."

McNally explains the difference between 2-D and 3-D movies by comparing them to other art forms, specifically painting and sculpture. "Traditional animation is a 100 percent flat graphic art form; story ideas are drawn in flat panels, and the final presentation in theaters is a projection of the flat graphic art. So it is like a painting from beginning to end.

"CG films are called 3-D because the computer builds them as a 3-D space. The irony is that even though these films are created in 3-D, the final film is delivered in flat projection. Thus, we are creating 3-D, but the end result is 2-D. It's like carving a sculpture, taking a photo of it, and presenting the photo as the finished work of art, instead of the sculpture itself. Obviously, the same could be said for live-action film, where you shoot 3-D people but project them flat on a screen."

All 2-D live-action movies have to create the illusion of depth without the power of stereoscopic vision relying on focus, tricks, and camera movement. Objects are set in the background or close up, depending on what the filmmakers want to feature in the shot. In 3-D, depth and space are inherent in the shot already. Thus, *Monsters vs. Aliens* was the perfect vehicle for 3-D, since so much of the film's visual component was about scale and size, two elements that can be terrifically enhanced with 3-D.

A good example is in the beginning of the film, after Susan has grown to 49 feet, 11 inches, is tranquilized, and taken to prison. When she wakes, she thinks maybe it was a nightmare and is confused. "Visually, we keep her close to the frame, and the camera work supports that concept that she is small, but only in close-up," explains McNally. "She walks out into the prison environment and we still play her being small. Then she steps on a tiny chair and, as she picks it up, we realize she really is still a giant. Then we switch and the camera moves to show her scale as a giant. We don't expect the audience to see that, but we are playing with scale and depth and 3-D amplifies what is already there."

For visual effects supervisor Ken Bielenberg, the 3-D element added great intensity to the film, especially in the "First Contact" scene. "The barrage of artillery in First Contact worked really well," says Bielenberg. "The missiles coming from the planes gave great perspective in 3-D because of their trajectory from

very far away to extreme close-up. Then there's a rain of shrapnel and plumes of dust. We had ten artists working on that one shot."

The 3-D technology can dial up (or down) whatever emotional arc or action the scene requires. McNally compares the technology to the musical score for the film, one of the many tools that enhance the theatrical experience.

Modern technology and advances in digital projection have removed the technical problems inherent in 3-D projection. "Hopefully, 3-D movies today will not repeat the error of the fifties by making too many movies too quickly, and we can build slower and more creatively," says McNally.

Clearly, DreamWorks Animation believes that this new 3-D technology is the wave of the future, not just for this movie but also for a long time to come. "Every character, every set, every single aspect of this film, from the moment we started making it, was designed to make it an immersive experience, to bring the audience into that world and to create more excitement, more scary, more funny," says Jeffrey Katzenberg. "This is not just a little trend that is going to come and go."

(above) **CG still**.

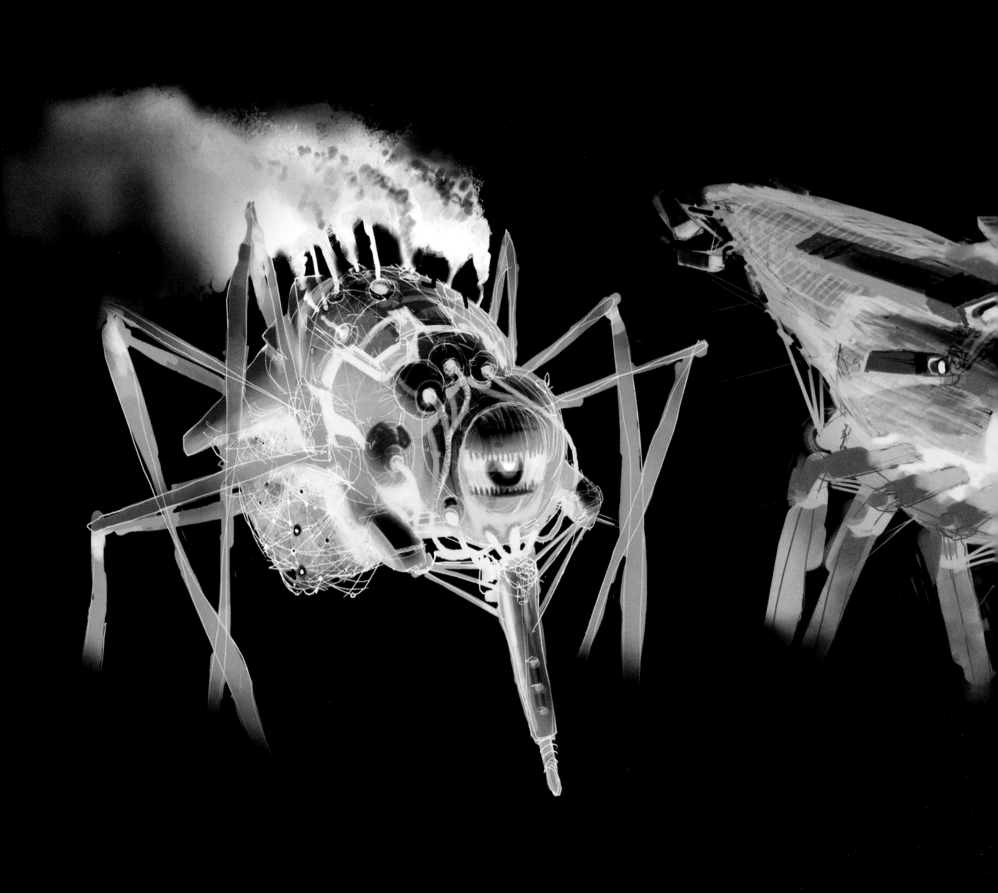

PART FIVE

OUT OF THE PICTURE

MOTHBALLED CHARACTERS AND LOCATIONS

In a movie as complex and innovative as *Monsters vs. Aliens*, there are innumerable ideas that are considered, discussed, drawn (or written), and then discarded for one reason or another. The creation of an animated movie is a journey, a learning process that requires experimentation and new ideas to grow and evolve.

Unfortunately, some of the best ideas and most glorious works of art get left on the cutting room floor or, more accurately perhaps, on the walls of the art department.

This book has featured a small sampling of the progression art for the characters and machinery that are included in the movie. However, there are hundreds of drawings of characters, environments, props, and ideas that never made it to the movie in any form at all. No look at the art of *Monsters vs. Aliens* would be complete without a peek at some of the works from the extensive "out of picture" file.

For example, the filmmakers spent a long time determining which character would tell the story. For some time, they worked with the idea of a monster hunter who gathers together the cast of characters. "He was an old guy who dies at the start of the movie," says Craig Kellman.

Then there was a red-haired self-help guru who was the focus of the story. "His purpose was to give the monsters self-esteem," adds Kellman.

(left) **Mothership Lagoon Concept**—Patrick Hanenberger—digital paint. *(above)* **Brain Planet**—Patrick Hanenberger—digital paint.

One of the ideas for the opening of the movie featured an invasion from a distant planet, where all the creatures were shaped like the human brain. This meant these aliens could say things like, "Don't get smart with me!"

An early version of the "First Contact" scene had multiple alien robots descending from the sky and landing on the Golden Gate Bridge. This idea changed once the concept switched to using only one giant robot. Of course, the design of the robot underwent massive design transformations. What started as a giant mosquito evolved into all kinds of alien shapes and forms. Ultimately, this design evolved into a simpler, rounder shape.

Patrick Hanenberger came out of one meeting with the instructions to draw eyeballs. "The directors said, 'Do something with eyeballs,'" says Hanenberger. He did. His early eyeball concept drawings would eventually morph into the one-eyed cyclops character that is the final incarnation of the huge alien robot.

No one ever knows where a great idea will come from, so the artists at DreamWorks are given free license to use their imaginations and be guided solely by their creativity. This kind of artistic freedom allows for the brilliant ideas and wonderful art featured in this book.

(left) **Early Alien Exploration**—Patrick Hanenberger—digital paint.

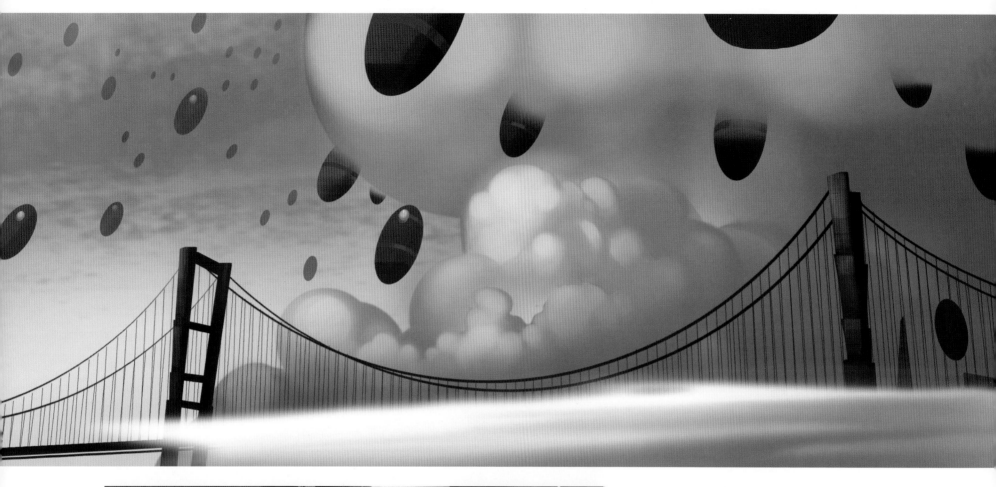

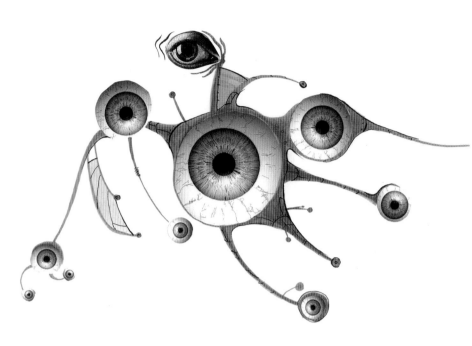

(opposite above) **Robot Invasion**—Ritche Sacilioc—digital paint. *(opposite below left)* **Monger and Tip**—Craig Kellman—character design—Richard Daskas—digital paint. *(opposite below right)* **Tip Sommers**—Craig Kellman—character design—Richard Daskas—digital paint.

(above) **Early Alien**—Patrick Hanenberger—collage & watercolor. *(below left)* **Monster Hunter**—Bill Schwab—pencil. *(below right)* **Monster Hunter**—Craig Kellman—character design—Richard Daskas—digital paint. *(right)* **Alien Concept Art**—Devin Crane—pencil & digital paint.

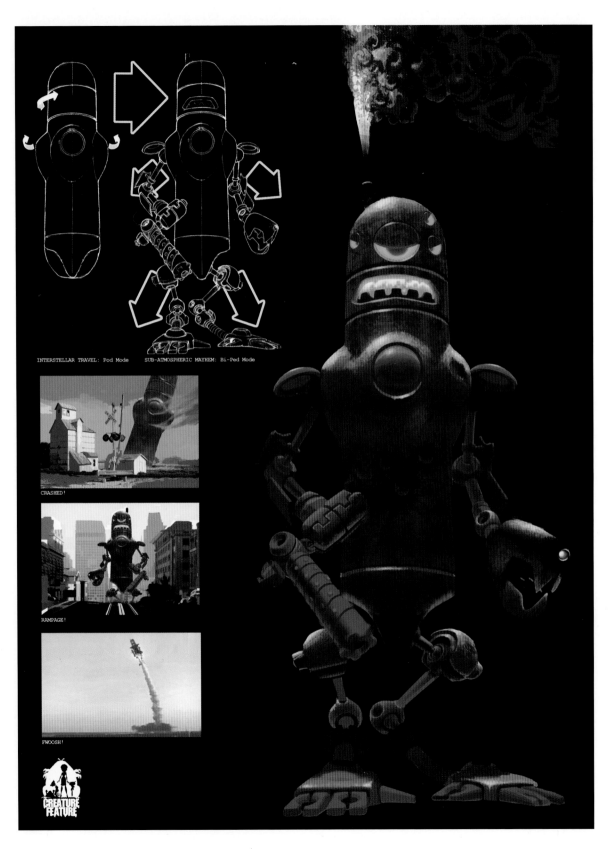

INTERSTELLAR TRAVEL: Pod Mode   SUB-ATMOSPHERIC MAYHEM: Bi-Ped Mode

CRASHED!

RAMPAGE!

FWOOSH!

(left) **Robot Concept**—David James—digital paint. *(top)* **Early Robot Exploration2**—Patrick Hanenberger—digital paint. *(above)* **Early Robot Exploration**—Patrick Hanenberger—digital paint. *(opposite)* **Edoterra**—David James—digital paint.

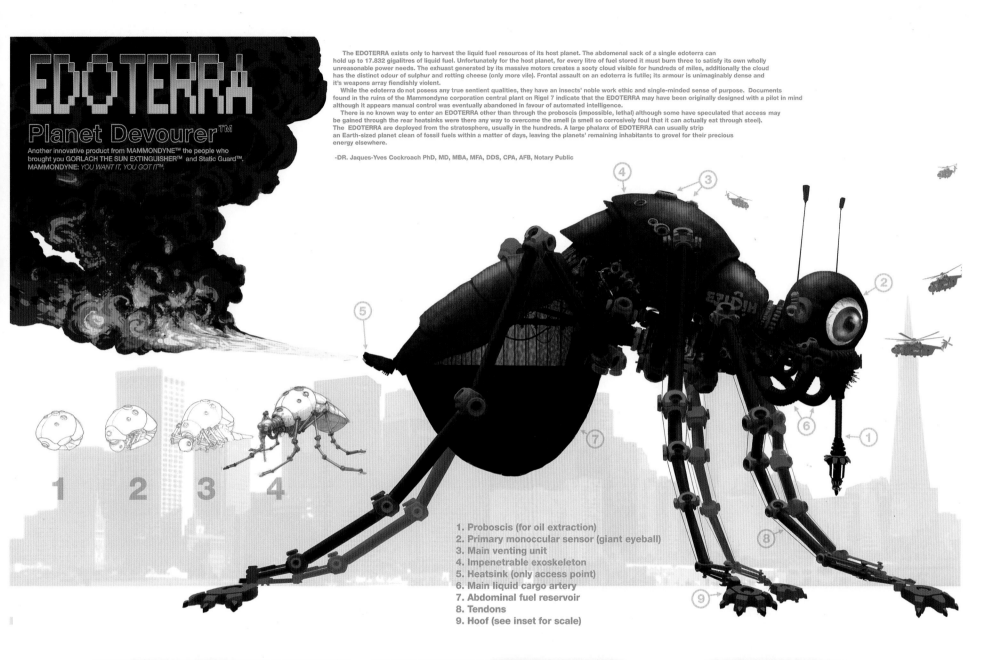

EDOTERRA

Planet Devourer™

Another innovative product from MAMMONDYNE™ the people who brought you GORLACH THE SUN EXTINGUISHER™ and Static Guard™. MAMMONDYNE: *YOU WANT IT, YOU GOT IT™.*

The EDOTERRA exists only to harvest the liquid fuel resources of its host planet. The abdomenal sack of a single edoterra can hold up to 17.832 gigalitres of liquid fuel. Unfortunately for the host planet, for every litre of fuel stored it must burn three to satisfy its own wholly unreasonable power needs. The exhaust generated by its massive motors creates a sooty cloud visible for hundreds of miles, additionally the cloud has the distinct odour of sulphur and rotting cheese (only more vile). Frontal assault on an edoterra is futile; its armour is unimaginably dense and it's weapons array fiendishly violent.

While the edoterra do not posess any true sentient qualities, they have an insects' noble work ethic and single-minded sense of purpose. Documents found in the ruins of the Mammondyne corporation central plant on Rigel 7 indicate that the EDOTERRA may have been originally designed with a pilot in mind although it appears manual control was eventually abandoned in favour of automated intelligence.

There is no known way to enter an EDOTERRA other than through the proboscis (impossible, lethal) although some have speculated that access may be gained through the rear heatsinks were there any way to overcome the smell (a smell so corrosively foul that it can actually eat through steel). The EDOTERRA are deployed from the stratosphere, usually in the hundreds. A large phalanx of EDOTERRA can usually strip an Earth-sized planet clean of fossil fuels within a matter of days, leaving the planets' remaining inhabitants to grovel for their precious energy elsewhere.

-DR. Jaques-Yves Cockroach PhD, MD, MBA, MFA, DDS, CPA, AFB, Notary Public

1. Proboscis (for oil extraction)
2. Primary monoccular sensor (giant eyeball)
3. Main venting unit
4. Impenetrable exoskeleton
5. Heatsink (only access point)
6. Main liquid cargo artery
7. Abdominal fuel reservoir
8. Tendons
9. Hoof (see inset for scale)

ACKNOWLEDGMENTS

The publisher wishes to thank, first of all, the wonderful artists at DreamWorks Animation who created *Monsters vs. Aliens*, and would like to acknowledge in particular the following people for their special contributions to the book:

At DreamWorks Animation: Ken Bielenberg, David Burgess, Kristy Cox, Devin Crane, Carolyn Frost, Patrick Hanenberger, Jeff Hare, Michael Isaak, David James, Craig Kellman, Rob Letterman, Yancy Lindquist, Phil McNally, Damon O'Beirne, Peter Ramsey, Jed Schlanger, Lisa Stewart, Vy Trinh, Kara Ulseth, Conrad Vernon, and Scott Wills.

Special gratitude to writer Linda Sunshine and designer Tim Shaner at Night and Day Design (nightanddaydesign.biz).

Also to the Newmarket team, including Frank DeMaio, Keith Hollaman, Paul Sugarman, Linda Carbone, Heidi Sachner, Harry Burton, Tracey Bussell, and Skye Senterfeit.

—Esther Margolis, Publisher, Newmarket Press

DreamWorks Animation Crew in Glendale, California